THE
MILLENNIUM
MYTH

D0964918

THE
MILLENNIUM
MYTH

Tom Wright

Westminster John Knox Press
Louisville, Kentucky

Cover design by PAZ Design Group
Cover photo © 1999 PhotoDisc Inc.

First edition
Published by Westminster John Knox Press
Louisville, Kentucky

This book is printed on acid-free paper that meets the American National Standards Institute Z39.48 standard.♾

PRINTED IN THE UNITED STATES OF AMERICA

99 00 01 02 03 04 05 06 07 08 — 10 9 8 7 6 5 4 3 2 1

ISBN 0-664-25841-7

PREFACE

This little work is a tract for the times. It brings together several concerns that have occupied me in recent years, presenting them as a single thesis: that to celebrate the forthcoming Millennium with integrity does not mean getting ready for the end of the world, but means challenging our prevailing cultures with stories and symbols that say, for our day, what the calendar we are following was designed to say in the first place.

Tom Wright

To the Bishop, Provost and
People of Coventry Cathedral

CONTENTS

1

Why Millennium?

We're going through with this thing whether we like it or not. The year 2000 is coming at us at the rate of 60 seconds a minute, 60 minutes an hour, 24 hours a day, 365 days a year . . . but by the time you read this there won't be that many left. The party's on the way. But why?

To answer that question we have to go back in time, and eastwards in space. Come with me to the ancient equivalent of Outer Mongolia.

The lands between the Black Sea and the Volga basin, and on to the East, were lumped together by the Greeks and the Romans under a general and loose heading. They called them "Scythia". Classical Greeks and Romans didn't know a great deal about ancient Scythia;

nor, for that matter, do we. Its inhabitants were generally thought to be warlike and uncultured, though not a great threat to Greek civilization or Roman power. Not quite barbarians, in other words, but certainly people from near the outer edges of the then known world. Scythia is at the top right edge of the maps of Herodotus in the fifth century BC, of Eratosthenes in 200 BC, and of Ptolemy in AD 150. It was indeed the ancient equivalent of Outer Mongolia.

In about AD 465, there was a flourishing church in Scythia; and at that time a man was born there with the very common name of Dionysius, the ancient form of "Denis". He became a monk. To distinguish himself from the many other Dionysiuses around at the time (people were often very unimaginative when it came to boys' names), he took the extra name "Exiguus", which means "small" or "insignificant". Dionysius the Insignificant went to Rome in about AD 500, and, despite his name, became in one respect one of the most influential figures in world history. He it was who proposed the new calendar, dating it from the coming of Jesus Christ. It is because of the Scythian monk, Dionysius the Insignificant, that we are to celebrate the Millennium not very long from now.

Of course, he got it wrong, and so shall we. Considering the material available to him, he did a pretty good job of working out Year 1 of the new era; but we now know that Jesus of Nazareth was almost certainly born in what he, and we, call 4 BC. Interestingly, for Dionysius the critical date in the year wasn't 1 January, because that wasn't New Year's day as far as he was concerned. Nor was it 25 December, the day when, according to tradition, Jesus was actually born in Bethlehem. No, he went back nine months from Christmas, to the day when, according to the same tradition, Jesus was conceived in Mary's womb. New Year's Day, for Dionysius, was 25 March, known to the church as the Feast of the Annunciation (when the angel Gabriel "announced" to Mary that she would be the mother of the Son of God).

25 March was, in fact, kept as New Year's Day for a thousand years. It lasted until a Pope, Gregory XIII, reformed the calendar once more in 1582. He it was who put New Year's Day back to 1 January.

Now for the puzzle that has foxed a good many people, and has kept arguments running in families and pubs. Does the Millennium begin in 2000 or 2001? People will tell you that it must be 2000, because after all when a baby is born they aren't said to be one year old until they've been alive for, well, of course, a year. So surely there must have been a "Year Nought" at the beginning of the scheme?

Actually, no. Dionysius did not include a "Year Nought"; his scheme went straight from 1 BC (not that he called it that) to AD 1. According to *his* calculations, then, the new Millennium will begin on 25 March 2001. 1 January 2000 is neither fish nor fowl; neither fully historical nor fully Dionysian. You should either have kept it on 25 March 1997 (and even that is guesswork, since we don't actually know the month and day of Jesus' birth or conception) or be going to keep it on 25 March 2001. The first of those days went by without much fuss, as I recall; and I suspect the second will as well. The wider world will simply see a new number at the start of its year, and will assume that this is of great significance. In fact, it's just an accident of our counting system.

What did it mean?

Much more interesting than calculating dates, and much more relevant for this little book, is to consider what Dionysius' scheme *meant*. To understand this we have to go even further back in time.

Two hundred years before Dionysius, at the start of the fourth century AD, Christianity underwent a great persecution instigated by one of the most thorough and ruthless of the Roman emperors. Diocletian, the emperor in question, was one of the greatest administrators, and one of the greatest bullies, the Roman Empire ever witnessed. He was also probably the greatest persecutor of Christianity in ancient times (modern times have produced, and are still producing, several rivals).

Diocletian claimed, and received, divine honors. Like almost all Roman emperors, he was worshipped as a god. He believed, though, that he was superior even to the other emperors who had gone before him; his rule, he thought, was the start of the new era of Rome's greatness, that would last on into the indefinite future. The Christians stood in his way, giving allegiance to a different lord, and refusing to worship him. Very well, he would systematically obliterate them.

Among Diocletian's reforms was the typical stunt of the serious megalomaniac: he introduced a new dating system, beginning from the year in which he himself had been hailed as Emperor, namely AD 284. He was neither the first nor the last to try this sort of thing. The last great Jewish would-be Messiah of ancient times, Simeon ben-Kosiba (also known as "Bar-Kochba", the Son of the Star) had minted coins in AD 132, the year of his revolt against Rome, bearing the number "1", to signify that God's kingdom was breaking in to the world. The revolutionaries in France in the late eighteenth century restarted the calendar, dating Year 1 from the time when, in their opinion, the Revolution had really begun (1792). In the same way, Diocletian intended all subsequent generations to date themselves by his rule. Self-congratulation knows no higher aim.

But, two centuries later, along came an insignificant monk from the back of beyond, and declared symbolically – and symbols are the most powerful way to declare anything – that the reign of Jesus is what matters, not the reign of Caesar. In other words, Jesus is Lord, and Caesar isn't. So, however we may quibble about the precise date, if Millennium celebrations mean anything at all, *that* is what they ought to mean. Diocletian the Emperor dated the world by his own rule, the ultimate rule of ruthless authority, administrative efficiency and brute force. If you stood in his way, he would kill you. Dionysius the Insignificant dated the world by the rule of Jesus, the ultimate rule of gentle but powerful life-giving love. When he finds you dead, he gives new life.

Consider the contrast a bit further. Caesar rules with the power of death; Jesus, with the power of the resurrection. That is why, and indeed is the only reason why, anyone would want to celebrate his conception and birth. It is because Jesus is the resurrection and the life that his birth is worth even thinking about. Take Easter away, and the Millennium has as much bounce as a pricked balloon.

How do you celebrate a millennium?

What then might we do to mark the Millennium? Even allowing that we're going to get the date wrong, in our public celebrations at least, what might be appropriate ways of saying in our own day what Dionysius was saying in his?

No doubt many countries have different ways of celebrating the Millennium. We in the United Kingdom have held confusing and unsatisfactory discussions as to how we should do so. Just as in parts of the United States people have become shy about even mentioning Christmas, lest non-Christians be offended, producing the bland "Happy Holidays" instead, so many on both sides of the Atlantic have sought to reduce, or even to eliminate, all Christian meaning from the Millennium and its celebrations. But let's be clear. If the Millennium is simply a secular party into which we can inject, or on top of which we can superimpose, one or two Christian bits and pieces, the whole thing is in danger of being a nonsense. This isn't Caesar's birthday party, it's Jesus'.

Of course, in a liberal democracy the rule of

"Caesar" is more diffuse, less easy to pin down. There is an important sense in which, if we all have the vote, "Caesar" means "us". But after many generations of increasing secularization, we in the Western world now have a society which regularly admits to itself that it has lost its way, and which actually elevates that lostness – under the name of relativism, pluralism, or whatever – into a principle, so that anyone who has anything definite and specific to say is regarded as a bit dangerous: someone might disagree if you say that, someone might be upset, so it's better to say nothing, or nothing very specific. Thus we have proposed to us in the UK, as the centerpiece of our national millennial celebrations, a wonderful symbol of contemporary Western society, constructed at Greenwich, down the river from central London: a giant Dome, that nobody really knows what to do with. In an article in *The Times* of London for 8 January 1999, the UK Chief Rabbi, Jonathan Sacks, contrasted it with the symbolism evident in the Great Exhibition of 1851 and the Festival of Britain held a century later. The Dome, he declared, "is probably the first great national symbol about which no one is altogether sure what it symbolizes." Just so. After much debate, it has been agreed that the churches should be allowed to mount a specifically Christian statement in it, but this met with much opposition, and its influence on the tone and content of the whole project is still quite unclear. We live in a pluralist society, after all. We don't want to be arrogant or oppressive. So we end up being . . . well, vague.

Actually, of course, it isn't so much the Muslims, the Jews, the Sikhs or the Hindus who feel threatened by the possibility of taking the Millennium seriously. Those who feel most threatened are people whose main creed is that religion is outdated and irrelevant, and that we can get on just as well or better without it. This is of course true, if by "getting on" you mean having the freedom to carve up the world the way that suits you, without being responsible to anyone or anything except your own financial end-of-year statements and/or your future electoral prospects. These debates about the Dome at the national level are reproduced at the local level, as committee debates about plans for the year 2000 become the playing field on which regular political battles can be fought out yet again.

Might there be a different way of going about it? How might we think our way towards the year 2000?

Let's take a look first at the strange speculations that have surrounded the idea of "the millennium" in the past. Another trip down memory lane. This may seem strange to us; but these speculations were ways in which people in the past asked the question: where is history going? What ought we to be doing to celebrate Jesus' birthday?

The thousand years of Jesus' rule

In the last book of the Bible, the Revelation of St John, there is a famous chapter towards the end (chapter 20, actually) which speaks of the great Millennium which is to come. Satan will be bound in prison for a thousand years; the Christian martyrs will come to life and reign with Jesus Christ for a thousand years. After that, Satan will be released for a short while, only to be overthrown at last, as the final judgment of the world gives way to the new heaven and the new earth. You need to read the chapter itself to get the full flavor, and to prepare yourself for the dramatic and apocalyptic speculations that it has produced:

Then I saw an angel coming down from heaven, holding in his hand the key to the bottomless pit and a great chain. He seized the dragon, that ancient serpent, who is the Devil and Satan, and bound him for a thousand years, and threw him into the pit, and locked and sealed it over him, so that he would deceive the nations no more, until the thousand years were ended. After that he must be let out for a little while.

Then I saw thrones, and those seated on them were given authority to judge. I also saw the souls of those who had been beheaded for their testimony to Jesus and for the word of God. They had not worshipped the beast or its image and had not received its mark on their foreheads or their hands. They came to life and reigned with Christ a thousand years. (The rest of the dead did not come to life until the thousand years were ended.) This is the first resurrection. Blessed and holy are those who share in the first resurrection. Over these the second death has no power, but they will be priests of God and of Christ, and they will reign with him a thousand years.

When the thousand years are ended, Satan will be released from his prison . . . (20.1–7)

What on earth – and I use the words advisedly – might all this be about?

There are many circles in which the phrase "the Millennium" has for a long time meant, not the turn of the year 2000 or 2001, but a great new age which will dawn upon the world, discontinuous with the present age altogether. There have, of course, been different theories about it, all looking back to the predictions of Revelation 20. A brief review of these may be in order so we can see where we are.

Many of the teachers we call "the early fathers" – the great Christian theologians in the first four or five centuries AD – expected what was more or less a restoration of paradise, following the return of Jesus but before the final judgment. This was a very much this-worldly hope as opposed to hope for a "heaven" which would be quite different from our present life. Many of these early fathers spoke and wrote in Greek, not Latin, so that these beliefs were (and still are, sometimes) known by the Greek word "Chiliasm", which corresponds to the Latin-rooted word "Millennialism".

Several other fathers, including the great Augustine of Hippo (AD 354–430), opposed this view precisely because it seemed too this-worldly. They followed instead the idea of a fourth-century theologian, Tyconius, who declared that Revelation 20 was symbolic, not literal: the "thousand years" was simply a way of referring to the whole age of the church, from Jesus' resurrection through to his second coming. The fact that a good many teachers of the church believed and taught this for hundreds of years after Augustine didn't stop an outburst of "millennium fever" as the date (on Dionysius's scheme, of course) approached the year 1000. This was not confined to the uneducated masses. The Archbishop of York urged his flock to repent before the Day of Judgment arrived. The German Emperor Otto III announced, "The last year of the thousand years is here, and now I go out in the desert to await, with fasting, prayer and penance the day of the Lord and the coming of my Redeemer." (Does this sound worryingly familiar?)

Augustine's view was predominant, ironically enough, for almost exactly a thousand years. Then, in the sixteenth and seventeenth centuries, the Puritans and others developed the view of a twelfth-century Abbot called Joachim: the Millennium, they said, would be an age of the Spirit, *preceding* the return of Jesus, not after it. During this time, they believed, unprecedentedly large numbers of people (including the Jews) would convert to Christianity, and bring about a worldwide reign of Christ, through the preaching of the gospel, before his personal return. This so-called "postmillennial" belief – because the return of Jesus was supposed to take place *after* the Millennium – played a large role in the missionary expansion of the church in the eighteenth century, and went with a largely optimistic understanding of God's work in the world.

This view, however, degenerated into the general secular optimism of the European Enlightenment, which gradually had less and less to do with specifically Christian hope. Partly in reaction, in the nineteenth century a very different view emerged, which regarded world history with deep gloom and declared that only the coming of Christ could change anything. This revival of "premillennialism" – the belief that Jesus would have to return before the Millennium could begin – has taken many forms, particularly in the United States. It is still widely believed in certain circles, in particular among fundamentalists.

Among the well known variations on this belief is the view that, when Jesus returns, the church will be snatched away to be with him in heaven, leaving a millennium – a literal period of one thousand years – in which all the prophecies of the Old Testament which have yet to be fulfilled will come true at last. This view, which forms part of "dispensationalism" (so called because of the belief that history moves forward in different "dispensations", in each of which God reveals a particular purpose and seeks a particular sort of response), holds that in this millennium the Jews will be restored to their land, and prove to be God's people in a new way. It is in this context that, among other things, many dispensationalist groups have seized upon the return of Jews to the Middle East in the twentieth century as a sign of the approaching End. I suppose we can expect more enthusiasm for this view as the year 2000 approaches, however illogical this may be within actual or official dispensational thinking (since classic dispensationalism has never actually claimed any special significance for the year 2000, or indeed 2001). We have here discovered the point at which millennial speculations join forces with rank apocalypticism, which we will look at presently.

All these speculations about a coming Millennium do their best to claim that they are reading and explaining

Revelation 20. At a wider level, though, they show the different ways in which Christians have tried, with whatever success, to bring together the idea of the rule or reign of Jesus the Messiah, the Lord, and the facts of world history, present or future. In particular, all millennial views stand for something very deep-rooted within the New Testament, found at the heart of the Lord's Prayer itself: the belief and hope that God's kingdom will come, and God's will be done, *on earth as it is in heaven*. What does this mean?

It is all too easy for Christians to suppose that "thy will be done on earth" is a kind of concession. While we're on earth, we hope, things will work out as God intends – but then, of course, we hope to leave earth behind and go off to "heaven", in which, naturally enough, God's kingdom will be fully present, and his will will be perfectly done. All God's people will be there with him, and earth will be left behind for ever.

But that very dualistic, very unJewish view has no claim to be Jesus' meaning. We should not be misled at this point by the way in which some still use the phrase "kingdom of heaven" or "kingdom of God" as though they referred to the ultimate destination of God's people – i.e. that "kingdom of heaven" refers to a place, called "heaven", in which God's rule obtains fully and to which those who are saved find their way. Far from it. As the Lord's prayer itself indicates, and as the rest of Jesus' teaching makes abundantly clear, the "kingdom of God", or "kingdom of heaven" (a reverent Jewish way of saying the same thing) is not a *place*, or a spiritual destination, but is rather a *fact* – the fact that God is ruling in the way he always intended. "King*ship*" is perhaps a better translation to bring this point out.

Millennial beliefs, bizarre though some of them may seem, are ways of trying to assert, with Revelation 20 in mind, that the Lord's Prayer will be finally and fully answered. God's kingdom will come, and his will shall be done, on earth as it is in heaven. Some have still managed to avoid the full implications of this, not least the premillennial Fathers (who still thought of an eventual leaving of earth and going to heaven) and those more recent premillennial dispensationalists who envisage Christians being in heaven while the Jews run the world on God's behalf during the promised thousand years. But the deep rumor that God's kingdom will embrace all spheres of existence, earth included, doesn't seem to want to go away.

Few if any of these views have been tied to actual calendrical millennia. Most have flourished, and have looked forward to an imminent millennium, well away from either AD 1000 or our present almost-millennial moment. No doubt some such movements will suddenly acquire a new literalism as the moment draws near; some may even wish to revive the interesting view, held by some of the fathers, that creation will last for six thousand years, corresponding to the six days of creation, before giving way to a millennium which will be the equivalent of God's seventh-day rest. (This was sometimes argued with a neat literalistic use of an early Christian letter, 2 Peter, which looks back in turn to Psalm 90: a thousand years in God's sight, says the writer, are like a single day, and a single day like a thousand years.) Since, according to the massively learned Archbishop Ussher in the early seventeenth century, the world was created in 4004 BC, this would mean that the seventh period of a thousand years would be due to start in . . . 1996. I didn't notice. Did you? Well, they will say, maybe it was wrong by a year or two. Maybe it really will be in 2000.

Actually, this is not a joking matter. Already there are sects and groups, in America in particular, who are getting together and making preparations. They are leaving homes and jobs. They are hiding out in the desert, prepared with plenty of food and water – and guns and ammunition. Their apocalyptic expectations are all too similar to those which produced the disaster near Waco a few years ago, and other similar events in which people have gone to their deaths under the deluded impression that the end of the world, the return of Jesus, the rapture, or some combination of the above or similar events, were about to occur. These manifestations of apocalyptic fervor have not gripped Western Europe to the same extent – there have been isolated occurrences, but nothing like what is happening in America – it is vital that, as 2000 approaches, we think seriously, and indeed biblically, on the subject.

Few such groups will stop to ask, I guess, why God should be bound by the decision of a sixth-century Scythian monk, rather than by the exact chronology which would have seen the moment go by on 25 March 1996 – or which would postpone it to the anniversary of the crucifixion or resurrection, which might perhaps be (in terms of Jewish months) 14 Nisan (some time in April) 2026 or thereabouts. Even a little historical information, even a few moments of reflection, might go some way towards defusing millennial hysteria.

But it would be a shame to give up on the millennial instinct, if I can call it that, just because some groups and individuals have got the wrong end of the stick. The millennial instinct, at its best, means simply this: the ineradicable belief that the creator of the world intends to rescue the world, not to abolish it. His plans are designed for earth, not just for heaven. When you put this together with the aim of Dionysius the Insignificant, who designed a calendar, however inaccurate, to proclaim that Jesus is Lord and Caesar isn't, this should give us a sense of commission that will more than carry us into 2000 and beyond.

What then should we say about the wild apocalyptic speculations that have characterized the millennial instinct at the approach of the year 2000, just as at the approach of 1000? To answer this question we need to address the basic question: what is "apocalyptic", and how does it relate to the coming of the Millennium?

2

Apocalypse Now?

Like a swarm of tired old bees, the elderly Christian buzz-words have not been buzzing too much recently. "Redemption" is what happens when you buy something back from the pawnbrokers' shop. "Atonement" is what a politician does when he (or she) is caught in some misdemeanor and has to resign from the government. "Justification" means lining up a page of typescript with no straggly edges. "Reconciliation" is what accountants do with columns of figures that don't quite add up. And so on.

But mention the word "apocalypse", and suddenly there's so much buzzing you'd think you were inside the hive trying to get at the honey. That's Hollywood talk. It means earthquakes, cosmic collapses, giant meteorites, interplanetary warfare. Special effects to die for. The sense of the whole world going into great convulsions so that a new world can be born.

It is no accident that the whole imagined world of apocalypse has increasingly become a fascination, almost an obsession, as the twentieth century has wound towards its close. There is a strong sense of crisis, of old things tumbling and new worlds waiting in the wings. We don't know where we're going, but it looks as though we're going there faster and faster.

This sense of an urgent race to we're-not-sure-where has been heightened by several factors. The huge technological changes in our world, particularly the explosion of information technology (you can now design your own virtual apocalypse, and that's just the start); the great political changes, particularly the collapse of the Berlin Wall and all that has followed from it; and the ecological changes of which we are now increasingly aware – all have contributed. Global warming didn't cause the end of the Cold War; that would have been taking a metaphor too literally, something which as we shall see intelligent readers of apocalyptic shouldn't do. But they just happen to have coincided, and together with lots of other factors they produce a sense of urgency, transformation, new possibilities and perhaps new dangers. All the stuff of which modern apocalyptic fantasies are made.

Of course, the end of the Cold War has meant that one particular "apocalyptic" scenario has receded – the possibility that two superpowers might press the wrong buttons and blow each other, and probably the rest of us as well, into smithereens. But that hasn't stopped the apocalypse-mongers from inventing ever more dramatic possibilities. And don't think we've seen the end of it yet. As we build up to 2000, and no doubt beyond, the race will be on to see who can devise the most lavish, thrilling, dangerous and dramatic end-of-the-world story yet. Novelists and movie-makers are queueing up to outdo one another in horror-fantasy futurology.

These stories, like most good dramatic ones, have all sorts of people keen to act them out. In our world, where many people find it difficult to distinguish fiction from reality (witness the gifts sent in to radio stations when a couple in a soap opera have a new baby), the Hollywood apocalypses, and the novels that mirror them, generate a real world where more and more people truly believe that with the turn of the calendar from 1999 to 2000 something cataclysmic is about to happen in, or perhaps to, our world. Nostradamus (a French astrologer in the sixteenth century) predicted that in 1999 a "great king of terror" would come "from the sky". (Of course, people have made wild predictions about 1799, 1899, and for all I know several other similar dates too.) A group from Denver, Colorado, going under the name of "Concerned Christians", have migrated to Jerusalem to await the Second Coming, and possible dramatic events that will precede it. With several such groups converging on the city, each with its own variety of prophetic imagination, the Israeli authorities have created a special force to cope with the resultant dangers. And in other countries, too, not least the USA, devout people from diverse backgrounds are taking drastic action to prepare for what they believe will be, if not the end of the world, certainly the end of the world as we know it. The Millennium Bug, the computer problem whose likely effects remain a matter of speculation, adds a bizarre contemporary twist to what seems otherwise a throwback to ancient superstition. It is perhaps typical of our culture that all these things can be put into the same melting-pot without anyone noticing anything strange.

Where does all this apocalyptic speculation come from? Why is it so powerful? Is there any good reason to link it to the year 2000? Are there any solid and lasting lessons to be learnt from it?

The irrelevance of 2000

The idea of apocalypse gets its punch, its buzz, from its biblical origins. There is still in our culture a latent memory – dim in some circles, sharper in others – that the Bible contains some bits and pieces which look like the special-effects script for one of those Hollywood movies. The sun will be turned into darkness, the moon into blood, the stars will be falling from heaven – people will tremble with fear, looking up at the sky, finding the world shaking beneath their feet. The last book of the Bible, which we've already mentioned in connection with the Millennium idea itself, is after all called "the apocalypse" (the word "Revelation", the title of the book in most English translations, is simply the English word for the Greek "apocalypse"). So does the Bible give any legitimation to these fantasies? Is it all true after all? Is the sea going to boil, as the old African-American spiritual says, and the sky going to fall? Will all this happen in the year 2000? If so, is there anything we can or should do about it?

Whatever else needs to be said, let us be clear about one thing. The year 2000 in general, and the transition from 31 December 1999 to 1 January 2000, has nothing special about it to link it to these fascinating but deeply obscure biblical prophecies. We may review the reasons.

1 As we saw in the previous chapter, the scheme we now follow was invented in the sixth century AD, got it wrong by four years or thereabouts. In any case, it envisaged 25 March, not 1 January, as New Year's Day. 1 January 2000 is a man-made date that just happens to look impressive within our culture.

2 As, again, we saw before, for the New Testament the most significant moment to do with Jesus was not his birth, but his death and resurrection. This took place in or around AD 30, at the Jewish festival of Passover, so its 2000th anniversary would be roughly 2030.

3 There is nothing in the Bible to suggest that the period from Jesus' coming, or his death and resurrection, to the end of the world (always supposing such an event to be envisaged by the early church), would be two thousand years. *If* the numerical systems of the book of Revelation were to be taken literally, and *if* the Millennium spoken of in Revelation 20 referred to the time of Jesus' present heavenly rule before some great cataclysmic event, then presumably that event would have taken place in or around AD 1030, the thousandth anniversary of his resurrection.

4 Millennial speculations have flourished in many times and places without any connection to a change of actual century or actual Millennium. What happens, it seems, is that the popular imagination, cherishing millennial speculations for quite other reasons, projects an arbitrary man-made time-sequence on to cosmic reality, supposing that there is something mystical about a great change in the calendar. You might as well suppose that your car suddenly becomes a different sort of thing when its milometer changes from 99,999 to 100,000.

There is, then, no reason whatever in the Bible, the teaching of Jesus, or Christian theology, to suppose that the year 2000 will see any kind of great change in the world. The language of millennial speculation comes from the Bible, but nothing in the Bible points to the year 2000, or its first day according to our calendar, as having any particular significance. If, of course, you believe that God can do whatever God wants, there is no reason why God should not do something special at that moment. But there is nothing that should persuade even the most devout Christian that this is likely.

But, we may ask, what sort of events should we be expecting, anyway?

Apocalyptic language

To answer this question we must look at the language the Bible uses at this point. What is "apocalyptic"?

It is a serious misunderstanding of the relevant ways of speaking and writing to suppose that when the Bible speaks of the sun and the moon being darkened and the stars falling from heaven, and of similar "cosmic" events, it intends the language to be taken literally. Four hundred years ago, the early English Reformers (people like William Tyndale, the great Bible translator) had to write careful essays explaining to muddled Christians that the Bible often uses metaphors; when it says that Jesus is the door of the sheep, for instance, it doesn't mean he is made of wood, or swings to and fro on hinges. They did this in order to free people from the tyranny of one particular understanding of the words Jesus used at the Last Supper ("This is my body . . . this is my blood"). I want to make a similar point to free people from the tyranny of a literal understanding of "apocalyptic". The word "apocalyptic", and others like it, have become notoriously slippery in the last few decades. There is no such thing as "correct" usage at this point. I shall simply tell you how I think these words can be used helpfully and accurately.

In common with many other scholars, I use the word

"apocalyptic" itself to refer first and foremost to a way of writing, what you might call a *literary convention*. Some writers chose consciously to evoke the cosmic or theological *meaning* of events in the space-time world by means of a sometimes complex system of metaphors. "The stars will not give their light", wrote Isaiah, "the sun will be dark at its rising, and the moon will not shed its light" (Isaiah 13.10). What was going on? Babylon was being destroyed, never to be rebuilt. In the prophet's world, that was like saying that London or New York would sink into the sea, never to rise. What language will you borrow to do justice to such an event? That of cosmic collapse, of chaos come again. The whole point is, of course, that the world has *not* actually collapsed; if it had, there wouldn't be anybody around to be shocked and awed at the fate of Babylon.

Take another obvious example, this time from the New Testament. "God disarmed the rulers and authorities", wrote Paul, "and made a public example of them, triumphing over them in the cross" (Colossians 2.15). What was going on? Jesus had been crucified as the climax of the strange saving plan of God. How are you going to invest that event with its full significance? Impossible, but one step towards it is to borrow the language of military triumph – which was of course all the more ironic, since in the literal space-time world what had actually happened was that the principalities and powers seemed for all the world to be celebrating a triumph over Jesus. The dramatic language highlights what the writer thought was the deepest meaning of puzzling events.

Take a third example. "Fallen, fallen is Babylon the great! It has become a dwelling place of demons, a haunt of every foul and hateful beast. For all the nations have drunk of the wine of the wrath of her fornication" (Revelation 18.2–3). This time, of course, Babylon is the metaphor; but what for? Rome, say most commentators ancient and modern – an interpretation seized upon the more eagerly, of course, within certain strands of Protestantism, and also, as I shall tell you in a minute, of Eastern Orthodoxy. Some, however, have argued cogently of late that the passage really refers to the fall of Jerusalem in AD 70. The debate continues. Here we have an interesting example. Unlike the wry comment made by T. S. Eliot, about having the experience and missing the meaning, here we know the meaning but aren't sure what the experience was. Such is life, and such, more particularly, may be some apocalyptic.

These three examples show well enough the main point to grasp. "Apocalyptic" of this sort is a type of language-game. It regularly involves vivid metaphors which enable the writer to say, and hopefully the reader to understand (Mark 13.14, in the middle of a passage most would see as "apocalyptic", urged "let the reader understand", though most still don't), the significance, within God's dimension of reality, of events that happen within our dimension, within the world of space, time and matter. To take Isaiah's stars, sun and moon literally – to suppose, that is, that he thought they really would be darkened and/or falling out of the sky – is as silly a mistake as it would be to take Paul's metaphor literally, and to suggest that the gospels have got it wrong, and that actually Jesus was not crucified, but won a military victory over Pilate, Herod and the Chief Priests. And, whichever city is referred to as "Babylon" in Revelation 18, the one place it certainly isn't is – Babylon.

That last example shows as well, of course, just what traps there are for the unwary in all this. Yesterday's literal statement may become today's metaphor; tomorrow things may reverse again. Nobody takes all the Bible literally, and nobody takes it all metaphorically, whatever they may say; we are none of us as wooden as our slogans suggest. In order to interpret any passage, particularly any passage of apocalyptic, the way of wisdom is to go through it one step at a time, deciding what is literal and what is metaphorical on the way. When Daniel says "I saw four beasts come up out of the sea" (Daniel 7.2), the "beasts" and the "sea" are metaphorical (the "beasts" are human empires, and the "sea" is the source of evil), but "four" is literal. When he says that "the little horn was making war on the holy ones and prevailed against them" (7.21), the "little horn" is metaphorical (referring to an actual human ruler), but the "war" is literal. And so on. This, of course, requires caution in serious Bible study, something that is not always much in evidence.

But all this, so far, is simply a matter of learning how to read texts from cultures other than our own; of recognising other people's metaphors for what they are. How does this get muddled up with the wild apocalyptic fantasies that we see sprouting up all around us at the approach of the year 2000?

Apocalypse and apocalypticism

The fantasies and speculations of which I have spoken belong, not to "apocalyptic" proper, but to what we may call "apocalypticism". This is a way of looking at the world, and a way of constructing or maintaining communities, which stir up and keep at boiling point certain types of end-of-the-world speculations. It is speculations of this sort that can, if unchecked, cause tragic disasters like that near Waco in 1993, when 79 members of the Branch Davidian cult died in a spectacular fire after a 51-day stand-off with the federal authorities. Some of the groups gathering in Jerusalem for the dawn of the year 2000 have links with that cult. This way of thinking does not necessarily cause such spectacular disasters, but it can produce various other forms of social and personal dislocation and malfunction.

Though I dislike technical terms in general, I find it helpful to use the word "apocalypticism" to denote the worldview in which certain people come to believe that their group is set apart from the rest of humanity, that it is righteous and all others are sinners, and, more particularly, that an event will soon occur which will sort things out once and for all. The sun and the moon will be darkened, literally not metaphorically; the Lord will descend from heaven and snatch the saints up in the air, literally not metaphorically; the Mount of Olives will be split in two, and rivers of fresh water will flow down to the Dead Sea, literally not metaphorically. And of course if you believe this sort of thing about yourself and your group, certain social practices follow: a tight drawing of boundaries within the group, a rigid exclusion of those outside, a carelessness or even downright rejection of most of the concerns of ongoing society, a focus on particular styles of worship and holiness. As history both ancient and modern will show, such groups are often internally fissiparous, fragmenting into smaller groups that then reserve for one another their bitterest anathemas.

Some readers of this book may be acquainted at first hand with such groups in the contemporary world. I am not; though I recently came across a surprising passage in one of the best books I have read for a long time, William Dalrymple's spectacular *From the Holy Mountain: A Journey in the Shadow of Byzantium* (London: HarperCollins, 1997), a travel diary of a pilgrimage through the monasteries of the Orthodox Middle East. I quote it here not least to show how beliefs the Western world has come to associate with one type of Christian group (usually extreme fundamentalism) can easily reappear, granted certain conditions, in very different ones. Dalrymple is visiting the Mar Saba monastery, in the Judaean wilderness of the Israeli-occupied West Bank. He is being entertained to a glass of ouzo by the monastery's Guest Master, Fr. Theophanes. Looking out of the window and down the cliff, he comments how beautiful it is.

'Beautiful?' said Fr. Theophanes, rustling his robes in horror. 'Beautiful? See down there at the bottom? The river? Nowadays it's just the sewage from Jerusalem. But on Judgement Day that's where the River of Blood is going to flow. It's going to be full of Freemasons, whores and heretics: Protestants, Schismatics, Jews, Catholics. . .'

'Actually, I'm a Catholic.'

'Then,' said Theophanes, 'unless you convert to Orthodoxy, you too will follow your Pope down that valley, through the scorching fire. We will watch you from this balcony,' he added, 'but of course it will then be too late to save you.'

I smiled, but Fr. Theophanes was in full swing and clearly in no mood for joking. 'No one can truly know what that day will be like.' He shook his head gravely. 'But some of our Orthodox fathers have had visions. Fire – fire that will never end, terrible, terrible fire – will come from the throne of Christ. . . The saints – those who are to be saved, in other words the Orthodox Church – will fly up in the air to meet Christ. But sinners and all non-Orthodox will be separated from the Elect. The damned will be pushed and prodded by devils down through the fire, down from the Valley of Josephat, past here – in fact exactly the route those Israeli hikers took today – down, down to the Mouth of Hell.'

'Is that nearby?'

'Certainly,' said Theophanes, stroking his beard. 'The Mouth of Hell will open up near the Dead Sea.'

'That is in the Bible?'

'Of course,' said Theophanes. 'Everything I am telling you is true.'

(p. 280f.)

We smile, too, perhaps, but the point is this: the Bible contains a good deal which, under certain social and cultural conditions, can suddenly mean very different things from what you might have thought – and, we may be sure, from what its original writers supposed.

The problem is that the New Testament simply doesn't support this literalistic use of apocalyptic language. For all we know, there may have been some Christians in the early church who really did believe that the space-time universe was about to come to a complete halt, to be utterly destroyed. Perhaps whoever wrote 2 Peter 3.10 ("the heavens will pass away with a loud noise, and the elements will be dissolved with fire, and the earth and everything that is done on it will be disclosed") expected it to be taken literally, but the last word of that quotation strongly suggests otherwise. It was only later that various scribes altered the phrase to "will be burnt up", which you still find in some Bibles. The point being made was most likely that a great about-turn would take place *within world history*, through which the secrets of all hearts would be disclosed, and God would be all in all. More of this presently.

I offer you as a summary of what I have been saying so far in this chapter a somewhat oversimplified suggestion, which would need a lot of further teasing out to be watertight, but which, within the limits of this book, may nevertheless point us in the right direction. Apocalyptic language, using cosmic language to invest historical events with their full significance, draws together the heavenly world and the earthly world;

"apocalypticism" forces them apart. *Apocalyptic language exploits the heaven/earth duality in order to draw attention to the heavenly significance of earthly events; apocalypticism exploits apocalyptic language to express a non-biblical dualism in which the heavenly world is good and the earthly bad.* To explore this further, we need to understand more about these two deceptively common words, "heaven" and "earth".

Heaven and earth

Here is a nettle which we must grasp if we are to understand the relevant issues that swirl around apocalyptic speculations, not least those surrounding the Millennium. When people hear talk about "heaven" and "earth", in our culture they normally assume that these terms refer to places at a great distance from each other. Many people still think that "heaven" is "way beyond the blue", a place up there in, or above, the sky. Even though most people know it isn't like that, the picture is naggingly resistant to serious thought.

Talk of "heaven" and "earth", though, comes to us mostly from the Bible; and in the Bible these are not two places, separated from each other by many miles, but two different *dimensions* of the total reality of the world. This is what I mean by a "duality", as opposed to a "dualism". Just as animals, and many plants, are irreducibly male and female, with the two being complementary, and both being good and necessary for the flourishing of the species, so "heaven" and "earth" are the two dimensions of created reality. These two God-given dimensions interlock and interact in a variety of ways, sometimes confusingly, often surprisingly. And it's particularly important to notice that heaven and earth were both created good. It isn't the case that the physical world is somehow shabby or second-rate, and the non-physical somehow morally superior. That is to move into dual*ism*, setting the two worlds against each other. Indeed, in the biblical story evil infected both spheres: creatures in heaven as well as creatures on earth, we are told, rebelled against God. But in that same story all things, in both spheres, are reconciled through Jesus the Messiah, though only after the principalities and powers, the spiritual powers that attempted to usurp God's place, had been defeated through Jesus' crucifixion (Colossians 1.15–20; 2.14–15).

My point is this: the *duality* between heaven and earth is very different from the *dualisms* of sectarian religion. The mindset that tends towards apocalypticism normally thinks of the heavenly realm, or the spiritual realm, or simply the non-physical realm, as always good, and the earthly, material, physical world as always bad. Hence the readiness to imagine the present physical world being blown apart in some great Armageddon, and the sublime confidence that "we" – whichever group that might be – will be rescued from the ruin in a "heavenly" salvation that has left earth far behind.

The question must be: how can we read apocalyptic language without collapsing into apocalypticism? How can we respond to the heavenly dimension of the world without lapsing into an anti-earth attitude? And, faced with the Millennium, how can we co-operate with what God intends to do in our world, producing earthly events with heavenly meanings? And how can we in our turn describe what God may be doing in our world, in such a way as to invest earthly events with their heavenly significance? How, in other words, can we do for our own day what the apocalyptic writers were trying to do for theirs?

Christian future hope

Before we can address that, however, a word is needed about future hope. Some, particularly those nurtured on lurid speculations about the future, may suppose that in questioning these interpretations of biblical texts I am denying future hope altogether. Nothing could be further from the truth. I attack the caricature in order to allow the reality to re-emerge from the shadows.

The reality is one of hope, not optimism. For the last two or three centuries the Western world has been nurtured on a belief in Progress. Despite all the evidence to the contrary, we have been taught to believe that the world is getting better and better. Industrial progress, technological innovation, and the many-sided wisdom of the Enlightenment, have produced and will produce a world in which old evils will be left behind. Try telling that to a Holocaust survivor, a Tutsi refugee, a Honduran peasant. Fortunately, their voices and others like them have now been heard, and, as we shall see in the next chapter, the arrogance of "modernist" optimism has been properly challenged by the movement known as "postmodernity". But where does that leave hope?

Hope has to do, not with steady progress, but with a belief that the world is God's world and that God has continuing plans for it. The signs of this hope within the world at large are not the evidences of an evolution from lower to higher forms of life, or from one ethical or political system to another, but the signs built in to the created order itself: music, the birth of a baby, the appearance of spring flowers, grass growing through concrete, the irrepressibility of human love. Some parts of our world simply point beyond themselves, and say "Look! Despite all, there is hope."

Within the biblical story, there are several moments that give particular focus and clarity to this hope. The Exodus of the Israelites from Egypt after their slavery. The return from exile in Babylon. The public career of Jesus, announcing the kingdom of God. And particularly, after his shameful and unspeakably awful death, Jesus' astonishing resurrection from the dead. From the very beginning of Christianity, the events concerning Jesus were seen as the fulfillment of the hope to which the Exodus had pointed. This was the real liberation. The future had arrived in the present. Hope came to meet us in person.

But (and at this point Christians and Jews would agree) the world has not yet become all that the biblical hope would indicate. We do not yet see peace and justice reigning hand in hand. The very first Christian writer known to us, the apostle Paul, wrestled with this question and came up with a clear solution. The hope arrives in two stages. Jesus' resurrection was the prototype, the beginning and the model for the new world that is yet to be. His coming out of the tomb into a new life was the personal, close-up equivalent of the Israelites emerging from their slavery in Egypt. The hope is that God will eventually do for the whole creation what he did for Jesus; God is at work in the present, by the Spirit of Jesus, to prepare the world for that great remaking, that great unveiling (that great *apocalypse*, in fact) of the future plan.

But that future, when it arrives, will not mean the abandonment of the present world, but rather its fulfillment. The whole creation, says Paul, will be liberated from its present enslavement to the forces of decay and death. You don't liberate something by destroying it. All the beauty, all the goodness, all the pulsating life of the present creation, is to be enhanced, lifted to a new level, in the world that is to be. There is no room here for the dualism that goes with so much apocalypticism. Rather there is a strong incentive to work, in the present, to anticipate the new world in every possible way. Those who are grasped by the vision of God's new world unveiled in Jesus' resurrection are already sharing in that newness, and are called to produce, in the present time, more and more signposts to point to this eventual and glorious future.

The central feature of the hope held out in the Bible is of course the personal presence of Jesus himself. Many Christians, not least those who tend towards apocalypticism, have reduced this feature of the hope to the belief that one day Jesus will appear, flying downwards from the sky, perhaps riding on a cloud. This event, the "second coming", is in fact the event for which many of the groups who see great significance in the year 2000 are getting ready, not least those going off to Jerusalem to witness it.

However, most of the biblical passages that are quoted in support of the idea of Jesus returning by flying downwards on a cloud are best seen as classic examples of apocalyptic language, rich biblical metaphor. They are not to be taken with wooden literalness. "The son of man coming on the clouds", in Mark 13.26 and elsewhere, does not refer to Jesus' return to earth, but to Jesus' *vindication*, "coming" from earth to heaven, to be enthroned as Lord of the world. (For fuller details, see my *Jesus and the Victory of God*, SPCK/Fortress, 1996, chapters 8 and 11.) And the one occasion when Paul uses the language of descent and ascent (1 Thessalonians 4.16) is almost certainly to be taken in the same way, as a vivid metaphorical description of the wider reality he describes at more length in Romans and 1 Corinthians.

Does this mean abandoning belief in the "second coming"? Certainly not. It means taking seriously the whole biblical picture, instead of highlighting, and misinterpreting, one part of it. The problem has been, in the last two centuries in particular, that certain texts have been read from within the worldview of dualistic apocalypticism, and have thus produced a less than fully biblical picture, with Jesus flying around like a spaceman and the physical world being destroyed. And if we really suppose – as, alas, many seem to – that this will be the meaning of the Millennium, we will miss the point entirely. Rather, the Bible points to God's new world, where heaven and earth are fully integrated at last, and whose central feature is the personal, loving and healing presence of Jesus himself, the living embodiment of the one true God as well as the prototype of full, liberated humanity. When we talk about Jesus' "coming", the reality to which we point is his personal presence within God's new creation.

The present challenge of future hope

What then is the challenge of God's future for the present? How do we rightly interpret, and re-appropriate, the apocalyptic hope?

The proper way of interpreting the great biblical hope is to see the present work of healing and liberation, the accomplishment of salvation at every level, as the bridge between what happened in Jesus and what will happen at the end. Deeds that truly embody justice, mercy, hope and freedom in the present are signposts pointing back to Jesus' resurrection, the ground of hope, and on to God's future, to the final presence of Jesus, the fulfillment of hope. The task, for those grasped by this vision, is so to act in the present that only apocalyptic language will do justice to the reality that is unfolding before us.

How, after all, can we begin to describe the full significance of what we are doing, when we plant a tree in a devastated landscape, dig a well in a desert, give hope and love to an abandoned child, or campaign for an end to war? Only poetry, art and music can begin to do justice to such things; the flat one-dimensional language of ordinary post-Enlightenment analysis into economic or political forces will remain earthbound. Like our biblical forebears, we need to rediscover the many dimensions available to us for describing what look like this-worldly events and investing them with their heavenly significance. We need to rediscover, for our own age, how to write today's equivalent of truly apocalyptic language: language that will speak of earth and resonate with the music of heaven.

This challenge, and this new emerging set of possibilities, takes a particular form within Western culture at this very moment. One of the features of our present sense of *fin de siècle*, of great crisis and transition, is that the dreams our culture cherished for two hundred years or more have let us down. The so-called "modern" world has been challenged in the name of something calling itself "postmodernity". This great apocalyptic upheaval in our culture seems to be going hand in hand with the approach of the Millennium; a change in the calendar seems to symbolize a change in the culture. The two seem to feed off each other. To understand the real crisis of the Millennium, therefore, and to begin to respond to it appropriately, we must take a deep breath and plunge into the strange new world of postmodernity.

3

The Way We Live Now?

So where do we think we're going, as the spider said to the fly? Cruising along in cyberspace, or merely caught in the World Wide Web? Stretching the envelope of reality, or simply living in a closed world of fantasy? Where is our culture heading?

I had better begin by defining some terms. Most of us are dimly aware that, as someone said recently, "reality isn't what it used to be". We are in the middle of enormous cultural changes within Western society, which leave many observers bewildered and many participants bemused. All the signs are that things are going to get more confusing, not less, and that the onset of the Millennium, which at one level has nothing to do with postmodernity, is making people on the one hand eager for and on the other hand fearful of great changes in the way we look at the world. The so-called "Millennium bug", the nasty cold that all our computers may catch on 1 January 2000, is, at the level of contemporary mythology, a wonderfully symptomatic disease of postmodernity. It is as if, in their explorations into cyberspace, they forgot to correct a ruthlessly modernist piece of equipment, so that when the new age dawned the computers turned into pumpkins.

But, in case some here feel left behind by all this jargon, what do we mean by "modernity" and "postmodernity", anyway? A quick thumbnail sketch is all we have time for.

Where we've come from: the "modern" world

By the "modern" world I mean, broadly, the western world from the eighteenth century to the present. The European Enlightenment at the intellectual level, and the Industrial Revolution at the social, produced enormous changes both in how society worked, literally and metaphorically, and in how people thought. The large-scale shift from agrarian economies to smoke-stack economies – from fields to factories, if you like – had profound social consequences. The philosophers who learnt to think for themselves without fear of tradition, and the industrialists who learnt to make things for themselves rather than having to grow them, acquired a new confidence: they could take on the world and do what they wanted.

Thus there grew up a modernist trinity.

First, the confident individual, master of his fate, captain of his soul (it was usually a "he").

Second, a certainty about the world, and our objective knowledge of it.

Third, and perhaps above all, a new mythology, the myth of progress, the claim of having attained "enlightenment" at last.

This unholy threesome was achieved by splitting reality into two. The principal fault line ran between "the eternal truths of reason" and "the truths of the empirical world", divided by an ugly ditch. Mere "contingent" reality – everyday facts and events that might well have been otherwise – could hardly affect the great timeless truths. But, while this might seem to leave the timeless truths in a position of privilege, that wasn't how it worked out in practice. Like the House of Lords in British politics, giving "timeless truths" this apparent position of honor was a way of rendering them ineffectual. The same split could be seen in terms of facts on the one hand and values on the other: facts were "objective", values "subjective", and there was no direct bridge between them (you can't get an "ought" from an "is", we were told). And, in the same way, heaven and earth, whatever they meant, were separated by a wall more solid, and more long-lasting, than the one which used to divide Berlin. God and humanity don't belong together.

The result of all this became clear quite soon: we were no longer bound to traditional religions or ethics. We lived (so the modernists said) in the real world, and religion and ethics were simply a matter of private opinion. Part of the avowed aim of modernity was to get away from endless European wars of religion, by showing that religions were simply about what people did with their solitude, and that it was therefore absurd to fight one another about such beliefs. We had learnt to think for ourselves, and could use this ability to show up barbarity and superstition, to free ourselves from the tyranny of tradition. Superstition, said Voltaire, sets the world in flames (he had Christianity especially in mind), and philosophy puts the fire out again.

It is this heady combination, I think, that people regularly refer to when they talk about "living in the modern world". Its positive achievements are obvious: modern medicine, communications, and hundreds of other social improvements. With a very few exceptions, such as the Amish community in Pennsylvania, we all live off the modernist achievement. Its darker side is not always so well known, but it includes of course the French Revolution (however much the aristocracy had asked for it, a movement of liberty, equality and brotherhood that kills thousands of people, including many of its own, to make the point is hardly a good advertisement for its own principles). The myth of progress and enlightenment created the context not only for Charles Darwin, but for that which followed in his wake, namely a "Social Darwinism" that made talk of eugenics, of racial purity, of selective breeding, and ultimately of "final solutions" acceptable, even apparently desirable, not just in Germany, but in Britain and America as well.

And those whom the Enlightenment enabled to think of themselves as "masters of their fate" and "captains of their souls" were of course standing on the shoulders of millions of workers for whom the main effect of swapping agricultural serfdom for industrial wage-slavery was the loss of fresh air. And, to pursue the political point, as European society has leveled out in the last two hundred years, it has increasingly achieved its new state of freedom at the expense of the rest of the world. The brave new reality of modernity, symbolized by the art, architecture, music, and politics of Europe and America in the first half of the twentieth century, has looked increasingly hollow. This is the context for the rise of postmodernity.

Christianity in the "modern" world

Before looking at that phenomenon, though, let us think for a moment of what happened to Christianity, and the Christian hope in particular, within "modernity".

It was seen, of course, as part of the tradition that had to be overthrown. In a world where objective facts were what mattered, the Bible was weighed in the modernist balance and found wanting. What counted was Progress, not Creation; so evolution must be right, and special creation must be wrong. Genesis was therefore out of line. Since science studied the unalterable laws of nature, miracles were out of the question, and half the biblical account stood accused of fairy-tale fantasy. Since Jesus was actually a Galilean revolutionary (or whatever), the idea of his being "the son of man", let alone the Son of God, let alone dying and rising for the sins of the world, must be the pious invention of the later church, on its way to the enslavement of the world in religious superstition. As for biblical ethics, they were quite simply out of date. That is an odd idea to apply to an ethic (one might suppose that if something was right, it was always right), but there it is.

Within modernism, prayer is simply self-delusion, sacraments are mumbo-jumbo, and God is a hypothesis we probably don't need. The Bible is reduced in its public role to being read as a piece of verbal wallpaper, and in its private role to providing holy thoughts for individuals to fill their heads and souls with (whether or not it's true). So strong has been the rhetoric of the modernist worldview that any attempt to show that these negative judgments were ill-founded has regularly been dismissed as attempting to recreate a bygone age. The tide of modernity is coming in, and anyone who questions it is a fundamentalist Canute. In particular, anyone who thinks there's anything special about a Millennium, still more anyone who expects an apocalypse, whether literal or metaphorical, is simply out of touch with reality. The New Age began, after all, in the eighteenth century.

But, as most people know, the modernist movement has been having an increasingly hard time of it in the last generation or so. Marx, Nietzsche and Freud, the masters of suspicion who were nurtured within the bosom of nineteenth-century modernity, have shaken to the core the modernist vision of reality and all that went with it. Their ideas have now given birth to a strong sense that all the well-known certainties of modernity are being shaken. There is in many parts of the world a sense of impending doom: hence all the fuss about apocalypse, which is being stirred up even more, as we have seen, by the approach of the Millennium. And all this is bound up closely with the cultural crisis that goes under the loose label "postmodernism". Again, the briefest of accounts must suffice here.

All change

The context for the cultural change has again been a change in the methods and assumptions of the way we live. A recent British Telecom advertisement, which urged "Why Not Change The Way We Work", suggests that we should stop commuting to overcrowded workplaces and do everything by phone, fax and modem (well, they would, wouldn't they?). Like most good advertisements, this one was telling people something they were already starting to think for themselves. The microchip has replaced the factory, the secretary, and a lot of other things and people as well; communities that depended on eighteenth-century ways of doing things have been reduced either to mass unemployment or to the status of theme parks, with the inhabitants now paid to dress up as miners, steelworkers or whatever, and to amuse the tourists by pretending to do what their fore-bears did for real. Instead of producing and making things, entertainment is the order of the day.

This industrial and sociological change dovetails neatly into the changed vision of reality that is character-istic of postmodernity. Instead of objective facts – hard-edged things, like lumps of coal or steel girders – we have impressions, attitudes and feelings, floating around in the cyberspace which all of us visit but few of us could describe accurately. As recently as 1967, the writer Gore Vidal could declare that "it is the spirit of the age to believe that any fact, no matter how suspect, is superior to any imaginative exercise, no matter how true"; but all that has been swept away as suddenly as the Iron Curtain. The change has been rapid, and con-fusing. At a conference in Dallas in the mid-1990s I heard a speaker give enthusiastic voice to a wonderful statement, trembling on the brink between modernity and postmodernity. "Today," he declared, "attitudes are more important than facts – and we can document that!" We have learnt, in the title of a recent book by Brian Walsh and Richard Middleton, that "Truth is stranger than it used to be"; that all truth-claims are made by somebody or some group, and that all persons and groups have agendas, which ingenious critics can smoke out with the help of a street-level wisdom that goes back ultimately to Marx, Nietzsche or Freud.

This is, of course, what preoccupies Western journalists, and not only when they have a president or princess in their sights. Ninety-nine per cent of the British satirical magazine *Private Eye* consists of the ruthless application of suspicion to all aspects of life. Only in today's cynical climate could the news that reforms at Westminster Abbey have quadrupled the size of the regular worshipping congregation, producing a nice problem about where to put the regular Christmas tree, be reported by *The Times*, on its front page, as a snub offered by the Dean to Her Majesty, the regular donor of the tree in question. Facts are not important; spin is everything. Every country, every locality, will be able to produce further examples of this. Reality is therefore no longer divided, as by modernity, into facts and values, or truths of reason and truths of science. It is whatever you make of it. You invent it as you go along. Choose your value and the story will follow. Too bad if unenlightened readers think you're telling them the facts.

Collapsing reality

Reality, then, is in a state of collapse. We don't actually know about the world "out there"; we only know about the inside of our own heads. This is, I believe, an old philosophical mistake that has now come home to roost, and makes its appearance all over the place. I came upon yet another example of it, trumpeted as though it were a quite new phenomenon, in *The Times* a couple of years ago, where Dr Dorothy Rowe, a well-known writer on psychotherapy, got on her high horse and angrily attacked modernist psychotherapy for its grandiose pretensions and power-hungry posturing. This is, of course, typically postmodern rhetoric – though it is somewhat ironic, granted that Freud and his followers were among the original architects of postmodernity in the first place. Psychoanalysis, having deconstructed everyone else's reality, must now itself be deconstructed. (Remember what happened to the original French revolutionaries?) In the end, she said, "We have nothing else other than the meaning we create."

Of course, this too is subject to the suspicious treatment that has by now become normal, though Dr Rowe did not acknowledge this. The dogmatic insistence that there is no such thing as reality except that which we construct for ourselves is just as much a dogma, an over-arching story, in this case about the theory of knowledge itself, attempting to impose itself, perhaps even as a power-trip, upon the rest of the world. Interestingly enough as a sign of the times, and perhaps of *The Times*, the same page carried an article about horoscopes and Feng Shui, the ancient Chinese belief about the significance of the direction in which houses, rooms and furniture face. The author of this article tried to cling on to modernism with one hand ("It is, of course, pure mumbo-jumbo: the kind of nonsense that for centuries has held back mankind and prevented individuals from achieving their full potential"), while flirting as dangerously as she could with things she regarded intellectually as superstition but whose evocative power she somehow could not deny. Here we have, all on one page of a broadsheet, the classic postmodern confusion. We know modernity hasn't got the answers, but the postmodern alternatives, though seductive, are either self-contradictory or unbelievable.

No more big stories

If reality is being merrily deconstructed, the same is happening to stories. One of postmodernity's best-known features is the so-called "death of the metanarrative". "Metanarratives" are the overarching stories which give meaning to all the smaller stories of our normal existence. Thus, for instance, many movements for democracy and participation within British society tell their smaller stories within a larger story of freedom that goes back to Magna Carta. When I was a boy, my world was full of cartoon magazines telling small-scale, human narratives of British soldiers fighting their own particular bit of the Second World War; these took their place, of course, within an implicit larger narrative about the war in general, and the respective characteristics of soldiers on both sides. Postmodernity has claimed that all such larger stories are destructive and enslaving, and must be rejected.

Modernity told an implicit narrative about the way the world was. It was a narrative that was going somewhere, moving to a climax. World history, according to this story, had been steadily working towards, or at least eagerly awaiting, the point where the Industrial Revolution and the philosophical Enlightenment would burst upon the world, bringing a new era of blessing for all. This overarching story has now been conclusively shown to be oppressive, imperialist, and self-serving. It has brought untold misery to millions in the industrialized West, and to billions in the rest of the world, where cheap labor and raw materials have been ruthlessly exploited. It is a story which serves the interests of the Western world. Modernity stands condemned of building a brand new tower of Babel. Postmodernity has claimed, primarily with this great metanarrative as the example, that *all* metanarratives are suspect. They are all power-games.

All we are left with, then, is a plurality of stories – your story, my story. You're OK and I'm OK (or not as the case may be), but the stories don't need to intersect or interact. Metanarratives are deemed to be oppressive; freedom consists in telling and living by our own mini-stories, our own local stories. This, inevitably, produces a world in which everyone tells their own individual story, often in increasing isolation. Nor is this the end of the process. The individual tells different stories about him or herself at different times, and even perhaps lives in various overlapping but incompatible stories simultaneously. The result is known, notoriously, as deconstruction.

Again, you can see this clearly at the political level. The post-war generation lived by the myth that world politics consisted of the Cold War, and that once that got sorted out everything would be all right. When America basically won by default, Francis Fukuyama wrote a famous article called *The End of History?*, declaring that there was now nothing much more to happen. We still, however, had, and have, the Middle East. We still have Northern Ireland. We still have Bosnia, Rwanda, the

Sudan, and many other places that no longer make it into the newspapers (the selectivity of the media is another major feature of postmodernity) but that have become running sores in our post-Cold-War world. The modernist myth about the way the world was was a cover-up. The big story of progress didn't actually stop the violence. (Nor did the little ones, actually; we shall come to that presently.) We scored the goal and found that we'd been playing on the wrong field.

The same is true, of course, with "progress" and "enlightenment" themselves. Everybody's liberation turns out to be someone else's slavery; everybody's economic boom turns out to be at someone else's expense. So all our great stories, our controlling metanarratives, are broken down into little stories: my story, your story, which may be "authentic" in themselves – this really is how we feel things, how we see things – but which will almost certainly not impinge on one another. (This is fine, of course, if we live in cyberspace, where we can create our own virtual realities, accessed from our suburban sitting rooms, but it makes no sense at all where there are real lines drawn on real pieces of ground and human beings get shot if they cross them, or happen to be born on the wrong side.)

This break-up of large stories into little ones goes back again to Nietzsche. He offered simply collections of aphorisms as the appropriate way to describe the world. We can see the effect in some contemporary novels. In *The French Lieutenant's Woman*, John Fowles offers a choice of endings according to the reader's mood. Julian Barnes's *History of the World in 10½ Chapters* provides no connected narrative at all, only a succession of images, with, as he implies, the "story", such as it is, like a raft adrift on an inhospitable ocean. You see the same thing in contemporary popular British culture in the rise, and phenomenal success, of the UK radio program Classic FM, which offers snippets of music, interspersed with the audio equivalent of window shopping, and only seldom indulges the older taste for a complete symphony, concerto, or opera. Break down the big stories. Put in your thumb and pull out a plum.

Who am "I", anyway?

The bottom line of postmodernity, as I hinted above, is the deconstruction of the individual. Nobody functions according to only one story. No longer are we the masters of our fate, the captains of our soul. We are each a mass of floating impulses and impressions, changing all the time, reconstructing ourselves as we go along according to the stimuli we receive, the spin that comes our way. As the jazz musician Charlie Mingus recently declared, "In my music, I'm trying to play the truth of what I am. The reason it's difficult is because I'm changing all the time." Observe that fascinating contradiction between two of the great postmodern agendas: (i) the need to tell *my* story, rather than anyone else's; (ii) the constantly deconstructing self. You can't imagine that sort of thing troubling Bach, Mozart, or even, dare I say, Louis Armstrong. The serious postmodernist would say, of course, that that's precisely where we are at, and that anyone who wants consistency is asking for the moon.

So the "meaning" of a book, a poem, a work of art is not something inherent in the thing itself, something given by authors (who do they think they are?), but shifts according to the readers. If metanarratives are to be killed off, so are authors, whose intentions remain opaque behind the text – and is there even a text, anyway? Isn't it just what I make of it? And if, in literary criticism, we have the death of the author, in all sorts of other fields we have a persistent and insistent attitude of suspicion, where Marx, Nietzsche and Freud have free rein, where all motives are instantly suspect, where there's not only no such thing as a free lunch but no such thing as a free gift. We are determined not to be taken in, and to be safe we make sure we aren't taken anywhere at all. You can see what happens easily enough if you transpose the same confusion into other spheres, such as politics, marriage and sexuality, or education.

This is the postmodern dilemma. Reality ain't what it used to be; the great stories have let us down; we aren't feeling ourselves any more; and we are left with a pick-and-mix culture, an if-it-feels-good-do-it culture, a whatever-turns-you-on culture. Sounds familiar? It is, at one level, the hippy culture of the 1960s come of age, all dressed up for the Millennium but with nowhere to go. This is true in architecture, where postmodernity really began; it is true in religion, music (Classic FM again), and dozens of other areas. Those who haven't heard the word "postmodernity" are nevertheless, day by day, confronted by the reality to which it refers. It meets us everywhere: in television, color supplements, supermarkets, and even (God help us) a certain amount of teaching in the churches.

At the personal level, the culture is symbolized by various noticeable innovations. An obvious one is the portable personal stereo, which creates for its wearer a private and constantly shifting world of sound. Another is the new-style pornography industry, which now provides safe telephone sex, or even cyberspace sex, for those who find that real relationships with real human beings are too complex, messy, or even dangerous. (My favorite misprint of 1998 was the tabloid which spoke of a certain American politician's proclivity for what it called "aural sex". I couldn't believe my eyes – or my ears.) At the corporate level, the great Dome being built at Greenwich as the British celebration of the year 2000 – a giant impressive space which nobody knows what to do with – is, perhaps despite its inventors' intentions, a near-perfect symbol of this confused, shifting, ambitious yet rootless culture. Welcome to the world of post-modernity, says the symbol. Never mind the meaning; feel the feel-good factor. You can make meanings up as you go along.

On the back of the revival of feelings over against facts, one of the most noticeable features of postmodern culture has been the renewed interest in "spirituality". Those who are still living within the old modernist sacred/secular split universe, and who became used to arguing the case for or against Christianity in those terms, are likely to see this as a great turn in favour of Christianity. This would be a mistake. After two hundred years of trying to pretend that we were one-dimensional material creatures, and that things of the spirit were irrelevant to real life, people in our world are now so hungry that they will eat anything. New Age mysticism, horoscopes, angels, nature-worship – anything that injects a note of divinity into our humdrum world is eagerly seized upon. We live in a very religious age. But this has little to do with Jesus or Christianity. Jesus and his first followers lived in a very religious age. Look what it did to them.

Postmodernity and the Christian message

What happens to Christian faith, and the Christian hope, within this culture? What effect does it have on attempts to think through the real meaning of the Millennium? I shall content myself with some notes on the way in which the postmodern climate has affected things; these, in good postmodern fashion, are random rather than systematic.

The first obvious thing is that the modernist critique of the Bible and Christian tradition is heightened. All great stories are suspect: the Bible is therefore not only politically incorrect because (supposedly) it told the wrong story but because it tells an overarching story at all. There are other stories, and these may be oppressive. We are reminded, for instance, that the Jewish way of telling the story of today's Middle East is now deeply damaging to the Palestinian communities. And so on.

The biblical view of reality is also, of course, under attack. Paul, we are told, saw things his way; but we should also bend over backwards to see things through the eyes of his opponents, who after all thought of themselves as Christians too, and may have had a point which Paul's rhetoric – the literature of the conqueror, after all, is what survives – has masked from our sight. Weren't Paul and the others simply manipulating their readers with cunning rhetorical devices? The biblical view of the whole of reality, which largely takes for granted Jewish-style creational monotheism, is also under attack; some have argued that the rather one-dimensional and puritanical monotheistic viewpoint we find in books like Deuteronomy was imposed heavy-handedly upon various other viewpoints, scrunching the little stories of the cheerful and interesting semi-polytheists in ancient Israel under the jackboot of a uniform, and subsequently canonized, monotheism. (The imagery is not chosen at random. Memories, and imaginations, of the tyrannies of the first half of the twentieth century continue to fuel the protests and the rhetoric of the second half.)

The standard Christian view of the person, likewise, will not do for the relentless postmodernist. If all God-stories are power-games, what could it mean to be made in God's image? Only that this, too, is a power-game, an example of speciesism in which proud humans project a glorified version of themselves onto the screen of hypothetical cosmic reality and use this to legitimate their rape of the rest of their world. Thus postmodern liberation theology, standing shakily on one part of the biblical narrative (the Exodus tradition), critiques other parts of the bible for their latent oppressive tendencies. (But aren't the Exodus-stories themselves oppressive to both the Pharaohs and the Canaanites, then and now?)

The reading which emerges from this is itself characteristic of postmodernity's pick-and-mix, smorgasbord culture. You read the bits that resonate for you, you give them the spin that suits you, and you use them to subvert the bits you don't like. When approached this way, the Bible becomes one cultural artifact among many, to be drawn upon when useful and dumped when not. If you want to read a text, why this one? One might just as well read Iris Murdoch, Seamus Heaney, or Jean-François Lyotard. Many do.

But suppose we aren't satisfied by having our understanding of Christianity, and of the Bible, conditioned by the present cultural climate? Supposing we are not convinced by the postmodern claims themselves, and not happy with the truncation of a lively and evidently fruitful Christian tradition according to the Procrustean bed of postmodern theory? There are several good reasons why we might either argue this point, or, in postmodern style, simply feel it.

For a start, there are the inner contradictions within postmodernism itself at the level of theory. To say "all truth is relative" only works if the statement, that all truth is relative, is itself *not* relative. It has been pointed out often enough that we are an extremely moralistic society, even though the issues we are moralistic about are quite different from before. The person who loses their temper at your inappropriate moralism if you object to their alternative sexual lifestyle will be equally angry with the farmer who hunts foxes to protect his chickens, let alone the developer who builds a new by-pass to free up the inner city. Heavy-duty moralism is alive and well; the rules have changed, but the rhetoric is as self-righteous as ever.

Even postmodernity's attack on all grand universal ideas itself becomes a grand universal idea. Its polemic against all metanarratives becomes itself a new metanarrative, a new Jack the Giant-killer, in which the bold young underdog hero (postmodernism) slays boring old Giant Modernism. It may deplore big stories, great metanarratives, but postmodernity has one itself. "The death of the metanarrative" is itself a metanarrative, wielding its tyrannical axe to chop the ends off everyone else's stories. Postmodernity, like modernity, and indeed like Christianity, is a story about history reaching a particular climax – even though, in postmodernity's case, this is a climax of despair: the Enlightenment offered a secular version of the Christian belief that history came to its climax with the death and resurrection of Jesus, but postmodernity offers a secular version of the old myth of *Götterdämmerung*, the twilight of the gods. Welcome to the postmodern apocalypse: the gods have let us down, and the cosmos will collapse with them. Especially if all our computers crash on 31 December 1999. This, too, is a story, a way of construing reality, into which everything else must be made to fit. It, too, is a power-play.

So we come full circle, to the anxiety, the sense of crisis, that seems to be converging on the fast-approaching Millennium. We don't know where we're going, and we're suspicious of anyone who tries to tell us. Some of the contemporary reactions, the current apocalypticisms, are blatantly ways of opting out, living in a fantasy-world, a reality constructed (in good post-modern fashion!) out of bits and pieces of apocalyptic imagery and Hollywood special effects. So is there an answer? Is there a way of addressing this crisis, a way forward through the postmodern dilemma, a way of celebrating the Millennium appropriately, and offering and embodying true hope for the world?

4

Making the Most of the Millennium

My proposal in this book is that there are ways of celebrating the Millennium appropriately which will help us find the way forward out of the postmodern morass. Once we understand what the Millennium might be about, we are setting a course for a restatement of the human project which will go beyond the questions and the denials of postmodernity and out into the new century with a fresh start.

The Millennium is, of course, a Christian festival. No Jesus, no Millennium; without Christianity the world would date itself, no doubt, in a variety of ways, quite likely linked to great political figures. We might, indeed, have a sequence of years, as in the Chinese system, which simply rotated like the days of the week;

it is a measure of the whole Judaeo-Christian heritage that we think of history as heading somewhere at all, rather than simply going round and round in a circle. And it is a measure of the stature of Jesus of Nazareth that many people who have never heard of him, and many more for whom his name is no more than an expletive, silently honor him every time they put the date on a letter or cheque. I do not presume that all readers of this book will share explicit faith in this Jesus; but I hope that, having read thus far, they will be prepared to give a fair hearing to a proposal that demonstrates what taking the Millennium seriously as a Jesus-based celebration might look like.

Let us briefly recapitulate what we have said so far. The reason we are to have a Millennium at all is because Dionysius Exiguus, fifteen hundred years ago, gave the Roman world a dating scheme which was designed to say that Jesus of Nazareth, the Jewish Messiah, is the true world ruler. In other words, in the language used by Roman citizens and early Christians alike, Jesus is Lord of the world – and therefore Caesar, the apparent ruler of the world, is not. The highly charged language in which the New Testament clothes its own similar claim has led some, at various times of history, not least our own, to suppose that the sovereignty of Jesus over the world means condemning the world to destruction while the righteous few are snatched to safety. The nightmare of this apocalypticism is, however, unwarranted by the texts, and by the message of Jesus himself and his first followers. They believed, rather, that the God who made the world still loves the world, and continues to establish his rule of justice and peace through Jesus himself.

If this story is anywhere near the mark, it can never be deconstructed in the way that postmodernity has deconstructed the great stories of modernism and beyond, for the very good reason that it is a story of love. It is a story of the creator's love for the cosmos, both in creating it in the first place and in taking risky and costly action within it to rescue it from its plight. Though our minds may boggle at trying to envisage what that love is like, from the very beginning Christians have seen it highlighted in the crucifixion of Jesus, understood as the greatest act of divine generosity. If this is true, this love is not subject to the critique of Marx, Nietzsche or Freud. Whatever else Jesus was up to on the first Good Friday, it was not a covert power-play.

Indeed, we can go further. It would be silly to claim Jesus as the first great postmodernist, but the grain of truth in such a suggestion should be obvious. Jesus stood for the love of God against the powers of the world. His parables were subversive stories, telling the tale his contemporaries expected to hear and then putting a devastating twist into it. They, together with his symbolic actions, were coded ways of deconstructing the great stories of empire that the Romans on the one hand, and the royal house of Herod on the other, were living by. God's kingdom stood over against all those power-plays. But the same stories and symbolic actions also deconstructed the stories of divinely sanctioned revolution, of holy brigandry, which many of Jesus' contemporaries cherished. Violence, he insisted, could never be the way of bringing God's justice, God's kingdom, to the world. That kingdom was truly, even if paradoxically, present in his own work.

Jesus' own followers assumed that he aimed at kingship for himself, and in a sense they were right. But it was a kingship so different, so subversive, that they could scarcely recognise it. Jesus was grasped by a strange and dark vocation, shaped by his reading of the Jewish scriptures and his own inner life of prayer. He believed, like many Jews of his time, that the great crisis of history – Israel's history, the world's history – was upon them. It was his task, at that critical moment, to take the brunt of his people's pain, and indeed the pain of all the world, onto himself. His own death would act like a lightning-rod for the great crisis that he saw coming upon his people, and upon the world.

This vocation only makes the sense it does within the biblically-shaped Jewish way of looking at reality, and even within that worldview it is shocking. But Jesus embraced it, and went to his death believing that it would be the means of bringing Israel and the whole world round the great corner of history, and out into the new day, the time when the creator God would make all things new.

The only reason anyone took Jesus' message, and his agenda, seriously for a single week after his death is because they believed God had raised him from the dead. Not that he had gone to "heaven", leaving his body behind somewhere; nor that he had been merely resuscitated, coming back like those who have what are technically called "near death experiences"; but that he had somehow gone right through death and out the other side into a new form of physicality, which had most of the properties our present bodies do but some others as well. The early Christians were as puzzled by this as we are – they had no ready-made conceptuality to handle the detail of such a thing, only the general belief that the creator God would one day bring justice and peace to all the world and raise the dead to new life. They were not ready for a dramatic action whereby *one* man would be raised from the dead ahead of time, bringing to birth a whole new mode of being yet to be completed. But that, they believed emphatically and unanimously, was what had happened.

The Jews had believed, because their scriptures said so, that when the Messiah came he would be the Lord of the whole world. The early Christians, who were of course all Jews, regarded the resurrection of Jesus as demonstrating beyond a doubt that he was indeed the Messiah; that Israel's God, the creator, had indeed been at work in him to bring Israel's history and world history to its awesome climax and out the other side; and that he was therefore the Lord of the world. And they said so, loud and clear, in a world which already had a Lord: Caesar, in Rome. They thus began the process – you can see it as early as the apostle Paul, twenty years after the crucifixion of Jesus – that would lead, five hundred years later, to the dating scheme of Dionysius. Dionysius hit upon a particularly striking and long-lasting symbolic way of making the point, but the point was as old as Christianity itself. Jesus is Lord, and Caesar is not. That is the Christian gospel message. The word "gospel", of course, picks up echoes from biblical prophecy; but it was also the word used by the Roman emperors to denote the "good news" of their own accession, or their own birthday. "Jesus – the crucified and risen Jesus of Nazareth, the Jewish Messiah – is Lord"; this announcement, and the celebration of this birthday, are at the heart of "the gospel" in the early Christian sense. To celebrate the Millennium with any integrity, therefore, must of necessity be to celebrate the good news that Jesus of Nazareth is Lord of the world.

Pause for a moment and reflect on how the Roman imperial "gospel" made its way. It was trumpeted around the Roman empire. It was a summons to live in the emperor's world according to the emperor's way of life. It was a call to worship; the Caesar-cult was the fastest-growing religion in the Roman world of the first century. It was a summons to allegiance, to loyalty.

Celebrating *someone else's* birthday as "gospel", therefore, was and is deeply subversive. "Another king!" said St Paul, and they threw him in jail. Absolute worship and loyalty, said the early Christians, belonged to someone other than Caesar. This, as we saw, was what Dionysius was saying when he invented the calendrical system that produces the current Millennium. This "gospel" message, this birthday news, is based on the whole Jewish story climaxing in Jesus, told as the healing metanarrative, the story of God's love. Christian worship celebrates and adores the God who is disclosed, unveiled, in the apocalyptic events of the gospel story itself: Jesus' life, death and resurrection pull back the curtain, disclosing the one true God of the world. Loyalty to this God demands that we reconstruct our symbolic universe around him, not around the gods who clamor for our attention on the street, in the media, and in the babble and confusion of our own hearts and minds.

Replying to postmodernity: the new story

Reconstructing a symbolic universe means telling the story; bringing the symbols to life; answering the key questions; and putting it all into practice. We shall glance briefly here at the first three, before concentrating in the last chapter on the fourth.

I have outlined the central Christian story in the previous paragraphs. The story concerns the creator God and the whole creation; it is focussed on the relationship between this God and the chosen people, Israel; and this, in turn, is focused narrowly and tightly on the one man, Jesus of Nazareth, who was declared by the creator God to be Israel's Messiah through his resurrection from the dead. In this man, and particularly through his death, the justice and peace which the creator God intends for the whole cosmos has been unveiled once and for all, offering renewed humanness for all who give him their allegiance.

This story then challenges all other large-scale stories of God, the cosmos and the human race. But it challenges them not as one power-play to another, but as the subversion of all power-plays by the self-giving love of the creator God. Those who live within the story and make it their own – that, indeed, is what is involved in Christian faith – have constantly been tempted to subvert it again, to turn the message of God's generous love into the means of their own self-aggrandizement. But the story retains its power, and produces, for instance, people like St Francis, who lived and taught a radical alternative way in the midst of the pomp and pride of medieval Catholicism; or, in our own generation, people like Archbishop Janani Luwum of Uganda, who faced the tyrannical Idi Amin with the message of God's love, and suffered the consequences.

Only when the Christian story is made to serve other ends, then, does it become the sort of "metanarrative" that postmodernity justifiably objects to. This is not to say that the message is comfortable or soothing. Those who hold to other worldviews, including those of other great religions, find it uncomfortable. The pressure has been on those who adhere to the Christian story to make it conform to the ideal either of the Enlightenment, according to which all "religions" are basically alike, and are all partly helpful and partly misleading pointers to the truth which ultimately lies beyond them all, or the ideal of postmodernity itself, according to which all religions, being simply different ways in which different people construct their own private space, are equally valid insofar as they help people to do just that. But the Christian story, with its insistent message of the creator's love, gently but firmly resists both of these power-plays, as it resisted those of imperial Rome on the one hand and revolutionary Judaism on the other.

It claims, in particular, that history turned its great corner, not in Western Europe in the eighteenth century (the more you think about that claim, implicit in so much modern culture, the odder it sounds), nor yet with the collapse of modernism in the late twentieth century, but in Palestine in the first century. That is the claim, of course, that our present dating system reinforces so powerfully: what the French Revolutionaries were unable to achieve, the redating of world history by their new age of "freedom, equality, brotherhood", Jesus has achieved through his life, death and resurrection. The

Christian claim sounds just as absurd from a modernist or postmodernist standpoint, not just because it feels unreasonable in general but because *it presents a rival claim*. The two cannot both be correct.

The Christian story stands or falls with the resurrection. It is the resurrection of Jesus at the first Easter that must be considered, from within the Christian story, as the real beginning of the real new age. From this point of view, any suggestion that the year 2000 will be the dawn of a great new era is out of the question. It can commemorate the dawn of God's new age; it can seek to implement that new age in new ways, a point to which we shall return. But it cannot seek to upstage the resurrection of Jesus. Only the final renewal of all things will do that, and as we have seen we have no reason to suppose that that will occur in the year 2000.

The story of Jesus thus constitutes the heart of the Christian "gospel"; this gospel is what the Millennium is all about; and this gospel is the heart of the Christian response to postmodernity. This story is not a power-play; it is the healing, rescuing metanarrative. To live within this story is to discover life and hope, new possibilities, new humanness, new openness to God, to other humans, to oneself, to God's future.

But how does one live within such a story and make it one's own? The answer is, as with any worldview, by adhering to the symbols which it generates, in which it comes to visible form.

Reconstructing a symbolic world

What are the central Christian symbols? The water and the meal: baptism and eucharist. These can and must be rescued from becoming commonplace and boring. They are the symbolic actions in which people live within the drama, the great earth-shattering play, of God's story with the world, with Israel, and with Jesus. Just as actors sometimes find themselves becoming like the character they are playing, so those who regularly enact the central Christian mysteries are forming their life-world according to God's story. "As many of you as are baptized into Christ Jesus", says St Paul, "are baptized into his death." And, again, "as often as you eat this bread, and drink this cup, you proclaim the Lord's death until he comes".

The great drama that is enacted every time these things are done "in memory of him" holds together past, present and future, joining Jesus' people with the roots of their faith in the history of Jesus himself, and linking them already to the ultimate future, the time when heaven and earth will be remade. Baptism and eucharist are "apocalyptic" events, moments when the veil is drawn back. Only the richest God-language and Jesus-language can do justice to the earthly events. The story and the symbols are the keel of the Christian vessel, keeping it upright as it charts its course through the swirling and turbulent waters of postmodernity and on into the next Millennium.

A further key symbolic action, often so inconspicuous as to be ignored, is *prayer*. As we saw, there has been a huge upturn of interest in "spirituality" in recent years, as the postmodern world finally turns its back on secularism's closed materialistic worldview and rediscovers the multiple dimensions of human life. Many Christians, tragically, have all but forgotten what a treasure they are sitting on in the gift and practice of prayer, and often don't speak of it at all, or only mention it in a half-ashamed aside. The result is that the world around, hungry for experience of other dimensions, looks everywhere except the place where, I believe, the fullest and richest "spirituality" is to be found: in communion with the creator God, through Jesus his son, in the power of the Spirit. This is not the place to develop a description or theology of fully Christian spirituality; simply to note that such a thing exists, is widely practised though largely ignored by the world around, and that while quick-fix books related to "spirituality" continue to flood the market, the deep hidden stream of Christian meditation, mysticism, adoration, thanksgiving, wrestling with the anguish of the world in the presence of God, and celebrating the joy of the world in the presence of God, is waiting to be rediscovered and explored. When that happens, a key part of the symbolic universe will be put in place.

Facing the questions

Story and symbol together offer answers to the great worldview questions: Who are we? Where are we? Why are we here? What time is it? What's wrong? and What's the solution? These, in turn, relate closely to the questions of theology: does God exist? What is God like? How is God related to us and our world? What, if anything, is God doing about the mess the world is in?

This is not the place to attempt even a brief sketch of the possible answers to all these questions. But we must note that addressing such matters, doing so with all the rich resources of the Christian tradition at our fingertips, and interacting in public discussion with other worldviews and theologies, will be an increasingly vital task as we go forward into the strange new world of post-postmodernity. There is an increasing danger that Reason will simply be ignored, and that arguments will become mere shouting matches where the loudest, or most acceptable, voice wins. Granted, the Christian knows that Reason by itself is not enough. The so-called "Age of Reason" produced revolutions that sent millions to their deaths; the Christian gospel highlights one who went to his death in obedience to a higher reason, the law of love. Nevertheless, this higher reason, sometimes called Wisdom in the biblical tradition, offers rich, deep and coherent answers to the ultimate questions, and we owe it to our contemporaries to wrestle afresh with the questions and articulate the answers in fresh ways, not least to rehabilitate Wisdom within a culture that is fast making a virtue of Folly.

The way forward

So what happens when the Christian worldview comes face to face with the challenge of postmodernity?

Christianity offers no support to those who, faced with postmodernism, are eager to run back for safety to some form of Christian modernism. The postmodern challenge to the arrogance of modernity is often well founded. But postmodernism is all law and no gospel. It's all bad news. The freedom it offers is the freedom of the isolated, random and undetermined atom. It is not the freedom of the children of God.

Let me take the three main elements of postmodernity and suggest what a Christian and biblical understanding might have to say at each point.

First, the story. I recapitulate what I said above. The Bible presents us with a great metanarrative. Postmodernity is bound to object: metanarratives are controlling, dominating, and we all know the ways in which this story too has been used politically, socially and personally to bolster sundry power-trips.

But the biblical metanarrative itself resists being abused in this fashion. The biblical metanarrative offers itself as the one story which resists deconstruction, to which the criticisms of Marx, Nietzsche and Freud are not relevant. It speaks from first to last of a God who did not need to create, but who did so out of overflowing and generous love. It speaks of a God who did not need to redeem and recreate, but did so as the greatest possible act of self-giving love. The problem is, of course, that the way we have reshaped this story has turned it into a power-play of our own. But the biblical metanarrative itself is not a controlling narrative: it is a self-giving narrative. It is not a power-play; it is a love-ploy. The fact that postmodernity cannot recognise love, but insists on deconstructing it, is its Achilles heel.

If we are telling the true story, and living it, we will discover that it contains within itself promises for deconstructed selves. We shouldn't actually be afraid of deconstruction; it points in its own way to the truth that Jews, Christians, and many others regularly acknowledge, that "all we can do is nothing worth". But what postmodernism never notices is that after death comes resurrection: the truth of baptism, as Paul saw in Romans 6, is precisely of new life the other side of death. Here we need, I believe, to develop as an essential part of the engagement between Christianity and contemporary culture a better and richer understanding of worship, the worship of the true and living God, by which we are renewed in the image and likeness of God. Those who tell the true story are invited to be neither lonely Enlightenment individuals nor shifting, rootless centers of impulses, but resurrected selves – here and hereafter.

In this light we can and must think in terms of reconstituted reality. Of course we must take on board the full weight of the postmodern critique of Enlightenment theories of knowledge, in which a supposed objectivism was in fact a cloak for political and social power and control. (The people who claimed to be describing the world were thereby controlling it.) But it is part of the essential human task, given in Genesis and reaffirmed by Jesus, that we should *know* God, one another and the world, and that this should be true knowledge.

Instead of the normal contemporary accounts of what happens when we know things (or think we know them), I believe we have to work towards a better one. Normal accounts of how we know things give supremacy to would-be objective scientific knowing (test-tube epistemology, if you like). Other things that we "know" about – literature, for example, or aesthetics – are seen as not really being proper "knowledge" at all. I propose a different way of describing how we know things. The deepest and richest mode of knowing is in fact love. Love of God is the highest "knowing" there is; love of human beings follows closely from that; and all our "knowing" of facts, theories, objects and so forth are variations on that theme. As in a good marriage, love goes to the heart of things. It opens up knowledge at a depth which no scientific analysis could either discover or disprove.

The point about love is, of course, that when I love I affirm the differentness of the one I love. Not to do so is of course not love at all, but lust. But, at the same time, when I love I am not a detached observer. I am passionately and compassionately involved with the life and being of that (whether a thing, a person, or God) which I am loving. I am fully involved in the process of knowing, but this doesn't mean it's all "subjective", that there's nothing "out there". Or, to put it the other way, though I am really talking about a reality outside my own mental state, this doesn't mean I am a detached, "neutral" observer. We can and must give an account of human knowing which starts from love and works outwards from there. And what better time to launch such a thing upon the postmodern world than at the Millennium, the time when we celebrate God's total and personal involvement with the created order, God's apocalyptic self-unveiling, God's knowing of us which brings into being a new knowing of God?

In ways like this it is possible, I suggest, to give an account of narrative, selfhood and knowing which embodies and reflects the biblical metanarrative itself. I believe that we can now not just tell but live out the story. I believe that the model of God's self-giving love in creation, covenant, judgment, mercy, incarnation, atonement, resurrection, wind and fire, and ultimately new creation can become the basis for our self-understanding, our life, and our vocation. And this inevitably projects us forward into the final key question: what should we *do*? What are the appropriate actions that will go with this story, these symbols, and these answers to the key questions?

Perhaps the most strikingly appropriate way of celebrating the Millennium, and thereby restating the

Christian faith for the postmodern world, will be neither the telling of the story, nor the enacting of the central symbols, nor yet the thinking through of the Christian Wisdom. The most telling way may be the actions that will say: this Millennium is the Jubilee for which millions have been waiting. To explore this we need another, and final, chapter.

5

Free at Last

The Millennium project that stands out above all others is one that embodies love in action for the contemporary world. Modernity says that what matters is the bottom line on the balance sheet. Those who work hard get rich, those who laze about stay poor. Well done to the first lot; the others probably deserve what they get. Postmodernity says that you construct your world the way you like it. But, frankly, that's a luxury which more than half the world can't begin to afford. They are far too busy paying for the world they've got – or, more likely, paying for the one *we've* got, as we stay rich at their expense.

Into this ugly scenario, which modernity exacerbates and postmodernity does nothing to alleviate, comes an old, old word from the Bible. *Jubilee*. It was what happened – or what was supposed to happen – every fifty years. Well, since we haven't had one for nearly fifty times fifty years, maybe the Millennium would be a good time to start. It would certainly say that Jesus is Lord, and that Caesar – and all the other power-brokers of our world – are not.

The Jubilee is of course not the only way of celebrating the Millennium. But it is one that people from many different backgrounds should be able to agree on. You do not have to accept the argument of the rest of this book in order to see the point of this chapter – though, if you have found the rest persuasive, what now follows should make excellent sense.

Biblical origins

The concept of Jubilee goes back to the book of Leviticus, chapter 25, at the heart of the Jewish law. Our word "Jubilee" comes most likely from the Hebrew word for a ram, *yobel*: ram's horns were used as trumpets, and trumpets were used to announce the start of the great Jubilee year. Despite the obvious association in post-latin languages such as ours with the root *jubilare*, and our word "jubilation", there is almost certainly no etymological link between the Hebrew and

Latin in question; merely a happy coincidence. Certainly there would be no greater cause of jubilation in the world today than a re-enactment of Leviticus 25.

The reason for celebration, as a glance at that chapter will make clear, is that in the fiftieth year all debts were to be written off, remitted for good. Our society has made debt a way of life in a manner that would have been unthinkable a generation ago. We have also now discovered that debt is a way of death. This is so for the student who is driven to suicide when a government's financial squeeze places intolerable pressure on her pocket at the very moment when academic and personal pressures are at their height. It is so for the struggling small business when someone else doesn't pay their bills, and the company, starved of legitimate income, goes broke. It is so for the homeowner who, faced with a sudden rise in interest rates, borrows more and more, gets out of his depth, and finally loses his home and, often enough, his family as well. We know what debt does to people. We know that few things will produce a cheer, a celebration, a throwing of hats in the air, like a large burden of debt suddenly rolled away. That's what the Jubilee was all about.

Some scholars suppose that the old Jubilee provisions were part of an idealistic legislation, invented late in

Jewish history and never implemented. Others, though, have urged that they are more likely to be deeply rooted in ancient Israelite law, falling into disuse through apparent impracticality under the conditions of the monarchy. However that may be, they form a tight and impressive set of regulations, not just as isolated rulings on a curious practice, but as an embodiment of Israel's deepest beliefs.

Put simply, the Jubilee provisions put down a marker which said that all time and space belonged to the creator God; that the creator God was also the liberator of slaves, the God of the Exodus; and that the purposes of this creator and liberator God stretched into the future towards his final fulfillment of liberation for Israel and the world. Thus, though there is a serious question as to whether the Jubilee was ever practiced by the Jews, at least in the last thousand years BC, the concept resonates on into the New Testament, and forms one element within the message and mission of Jesus as remembered by the early church.

The Jubilee, then, was designed to function as a signpost reminding the people of Israel where they had come from and where they were going to. It looked back to the Exodus, when the Jewish people were constituted precisely as God's freed slaves; and it looked on to the promised time when everyone would sit under their own vines and fig trees, and none would make them afraid. In doing this, it also drew together land and family, both fundamental constitutive symbols of Jewish identity. It was another of those events designed to function apocalyptically, revealing the true God within space-time affairs. If all your heaviest debts were suddenly rolled away, you would reach for vivid, almost cosmic, metaphors to express the meaning of the event.

Basic to Leviticus 25 was the belief that YHWH, Israel's God, was the actual owner of the land of Israel, and indeed of all the earth. Those who "owned" land in the ordinary human way did so as God's tenants. Every harvest, and the festivals that went with them, reminded the Israelites that they owed their existence as free people to their God, and were under obligation to act towards one another as their God had acted towards them. This sense of stewardship, still retained by many people throughout our world, is of course mocked and trampled upon by those who, with the modernist imperative as their watchword, look at a piece of land and only see economic possibilities. Leviticus reminds us of an older way, all but forgotten in the post-eighteenth century Northern hemisphere.

The key feature of the chapter, flowing from this, is the central belief that the land should remain under the ownership of the same clan and, within that, the same family. Family land was to be ultimately inalienable. The detailed case-law which implements these principles has one great aim in view: that no Israelite will ever be reduced, together with his dependents, to perpetual penury. The Jubilee was a way of ensuring that families could go on living on their land, that the fragile fabric of society would be preserved, with individual families and the community at large living in a viable and interdependent balance. It was thus aimed at maintaining the socio-economic basis of the nation's covenant relationship with her God.

Whether or not this provision was ever applied in practice, it provided part of the future hope articulated by some of Israel's greatest prophets. Famously, chapter 61 of the book of the prophet Isaiah sums up a good deal of the prophetic critique of Israel, and the summons to a faith and hope which embrace the principle of the Exodus, by announcing "The year of YHWH's favour", including "release for the captives".

The prophet was referring to the ultimate restoration of God's people. But the wider context of chapter 61 includes several strong appeals for social justice in the present. Here is a great lesson to learn, and implement, in the Millennium. God's intended future is not merely an idealistic dream, but is rooted in his character as the liberator, and his past deeds of liberation, supremely the Exodus. Because of this, Israel was summoned to practice *in the present time*, as far as possible, those social conditions which would anticipate what God intended to accomplish at the end. And if they, how much more we; if then, how much more now.

With all this in mind, we turn to the New Testament. Christians have long been accustomed to regard the New Testament as dealing with "spiritual" rather than practical, social or economic matters; but this is a misapprehension, based particularly on the Enlightenment's insistence on splitting religion and politics apart and then on reading this split back into the Bible. In fact, as is well known, Jesus in his so-called "Nazareth Manifesto" (Luke 4) announced a program which explicitly picked up the theme of Isaiah 61, speaking of liberation for the captives and the year of the Lord's favour.

In this light, we shouldn't be surprised when we meet the same theme in other parts of Jesus' teaching. In the Lord's prayer, and in Jesus' wider teaching, it would be wrong to assume that "forgiveness" always and only means forgiveness of moral faults or personal hurts. "Forgive us our debts, as we forgive our debtors": this forms part of the program announced by, and indeed subsumed under, the general petition, "Thy kingdom come, thy will be done, in earth as in heaven". When Jesus told a story about a man who had been forgiven a huge debt and then sued a neighbor for a tiny one (Matthew 18), this was not only an illustration of abstract forgiveness. Israel was supposed to be the nation of freed slaves, who celebrated their freedom by sharing it. Jesus was calling his followers to be true Israelites, forgiving one another debts of all sorts.

I don't think Jesus thought his contemporaries would actually implement the Jubilee at a national level. But it seems to me clear that he wanted his followers, those who heard his message and responded to it during his lifetime, to live as cells of Jubilee people, witnessing to Israel as a whole that there was a different way of being Israel, a way which went back to the roots, back to the God of justice and mercy. It appears from the Acts of the Apostles that his first followers took this very seriously. They lived together as a community in which everything was shared and none were in want.

Celebrating the lordship of Jesus

Where does all this take us? Some religions believe in a strict, blind justice, in which all creatures reap what they sow, coming back into different embodiments to receive their just deserts. Christianity from the first, with its roots deep in biblical Judaism, has been a religion of forgiveness, of new starts, of wiping the slate clean at every level. When, at his crucifixion, Jesus prayed "Father, forgive them; they do not know what they are doing", his words carried, of course, immediate relevance to those who were nailing him to the cross. But his meaning echoes out far wider into the world of unforgiveness, of deeper and deeper indebtedness. Our post-Enlightenment society often lives by the rule of self-help, pulling oneself up by one's moral, spiritual, sociological or economic bootstraps. Christianity is all about grace, about mercy reaching those who can't help themselves, about forgiveness and new starts for those who could never make it by themselves.

Christians believe that in Jesus, the Messiah, the purposes of the creator God for his people Israel reached their glorious climax, the real and full Exodus. So those who give allegiance to Jesus, and indeed those who merely glimpse that in him there might be a new way forward for the world as a whole, have an opportunity, and perhaps even an obligation, to work out the ways in which Old Testament laws can appropriately be translated into the world of the New. Christians believe that the people of God consists now, not of one nation only, but of all those who believe in the one true creator God, the God of Israel, revealed in Jesus the Messiah, the Lord of the world. Because in Jesus' resurrection and ascension we see the triumph of God over all the forces of evil, we acclaim Jesus as Lord, sovereign over all other lords. Jesus is Lord, therefore Caesar isn't; Jesus is Lord, therefore Mammon isn't; Jesus is Lord, therefore Marx isn't, Freud isn't, Nietzsche isn't: money, sex and power, the great gods of our age and perhaps every age, are dethroned by the crucified and risen Lord of all the earth. Celebrating the Millennium is also about giving the right answer to postmodernity. In the resurrection Jesus has become the Jubilee in person, the liberated liberator. Being himself freed from the chains of death, he now lives to free others from all that enslaves them.

To believe this is also to believe that the final complete liberation promised by Jesus – the resurrection life and all that it entails – is not simply to be confined to a distant or post mortem future, but is to be anticipated in the here and now. Thy kingdom come, Jesus taught his followers to pray, *on earth as it is in heaven.* The Jews looked back to the Exodus and on to the Messianic age, and, in theory at least, they kept the Jubilee as a signpost on that road, the road to freedom for the freedom-people. So those who believe that we live in the Messianic age, between the death and resurrection of Jesus on the one hand and the final restoration of all things on the other, must put up signposts to remind them that they are on that journey.

The greatest of these signposts are, as we saw, the sacraments of baptism and eucharist. But there are all sorts of other signposts which make the same point symbolically and practically. Jubilee, the release of debts, is certainly one such. Nearer home, we live in a tradition that saw, in the last century, the freeing of the slaves as a great sign of Christian witness, achieved only after a long and sometimes bitter struggle (in which, alas, the church was often on the wrong side). It is now time, in our generation, to go back to the book, and forward in hope: to raise the signpost that speaks of liberation and jubilee.

It will not be easy or cheap. God's victories never are. But to settle for anything less would be to retreat, as the Enlightenment desperately wanted us to, into the purely private sphere; to collude with the powers that Jesus defeated on the cross; to withdraw the claim that the crucified and risen Jesus is the Lord of the whole world. If we give that up we might as well not celebrate the Millennium at all. If we abandon the claim of Jesus, we have no answer to the cynicism and despair of post-modernity. This belief about Jesus, after all, is what prevents apocalyptic from sliding into apocalypticism. Christian responsibility to the wider world, when properly grasped, prevents Jesus' followers from becoming a defensive little sect, and summons them to live for their neighbors in the global village.

Jubilee 2000: the need and the project

We are now in a position to home in on a project which brings a truly Christian, indeed apocalyptic, millennial vision to bear upon today's postmodern world. This project tells the story of the whole human race as a story of freedom from slavery. It answers the worldview question, Who are we?, with the news that we human beings are not only made for freedom, but made to give that freedom to each other. It plants the symbol that says Jesus is Lord, and mighty Mammon is not. It puts into practice the imperative of self-giving love. The project is called, quite simply: Jubilee 2000.

Jubilee 2000 is the answer to the cry for help that comes from millions of desperate children, women and men throughout our world. They are enslaved, almost all through no fault of their own – unless you count being born in the wrong place at the wrong time. They are enslaved to debt; which is of course an oblique and polite way of saying that they are enslaved to those who have lent them money. In other words, to the economically powerful nations, to which most of those who read this book will belong. The Jubilee 2000 movement offers a clear, workable proposal calling for a one-off cancellation, by the year 2000, of the backlog of unpayable debt owed by the world's poorest countries, under a fair and transparent process. Information about the movement can be obtained from one of the addresses in the Appendix at the end of this book.

International debt is something most thinking people know a little about, but few have stopped to ponder its full weight and implications. Lending institutions, from the World Bank downwards, have lent enormous sums of money to the nations in the two-thirds world. Countries in Latin America owe over £400 billion – roughly $640 billion US – to the world's richest nations and financial institutions. Sub-Saharan Africa owes more than £135 billion ($216 billion). These debts began as easy credit at a time when interest rates were low; many governments were lured into them with attractive offers and special terms. But, as individuals often find, the lender who smiles so enticingly when offering money up front frowns severely when payment becomes difficult.

And payment in many cases is next to impossible. Africa now spends twice as much on debt repayments as on health care. Millions of lives could be saved if that money was put into education, health, clean water and sanitation. The UNDP Human Development Report, published in 1997, estimated that debt relief by the year 2000 could save the lives of 21 million children. Children, indeed, are the most vulnerable victims: in the poorest countries, malnutrition and infant mortality are on the increase, while school attendance and educational standards are on the decline. Mozambique spends four times more in loan interest than on health care. Zambia spends five times more on debt than on education. All this could be changed very quickly if the huge burden of debt were removed.

Even to service the debt (i.e. to pay the interest on it) is beyond the power of many of the countries worst affected. Since there is no international bankruptcy law, the massive loans that were made many years ago simply accumulate interest, and interest on interest. Some countries have already paid back two or three times the original amount of the loan, but they still find their debt is growing. The organization called Comic Relief raised £26 million ($42 million) in 1997. That sounds quite impressive, but Africa hands over that amount in debt repayments *every single day*. The rich nations of the world give a certain amount in aid to the poorer ones. But for every pound, or dollar, given in this way, another *nine* are claimed back in debt repayments, much of it accumulated interest.

It is easy for people in the West to blame the borrowers for over-extending themselves. But even if those who are now paying were responsible for the original debt, which is usually not the case, this would be a burden far too heavy for one human being, or country, to lay on another. In fact, many loans were undertaken by tyrants who used the money for their own pleasure and who now, having been toppled, have left their subjects, who never benefited from the money in the first place, to pay it back. Loans were often given by governments or government-backed organizations to prop up politically useful dictators, and to promote Western business interests abroad. Ninety-five per cent of the debts owed to the UK are for loans used to promote UK trade, especially arms; in other words, we lent them the money to buy our deadly products, and now, having made the sale, we are charging them interest on it as well.

A further unpleasant twist in the tale emerges when we consider the implications of how repayment is made. Debts must be paid in hard currency, and that means dollars. As world prices for exported goods fall, demand for more dollars to pay the debt encourages such activities as illegal drug smuggling and the destruction of rainforests. Anything to get more of the magic hard currency. These nations desperately need the chance to develop healthy and ecologically appropriate economies, instead of living from hand to mouth and taking what they can where they can irrespective of the consequences.

Of course there will be powerful vested interests who will say that remission of debt is either impossible or plain wrong. Some will warn that debt cancellation without political change will be a gift to the tyrants and bullies, not to the poor and weak. Steps will have to be taken to make sure that unpayable debts never build up again, and that cancellation benefits the people it is designed to, rather than giving already rich tyrants a further free ride. But the fact that care has to be taken is not a good reason for doing nothing. It is easy to forget that the West German economic renaissance after the Second World War was directly caused by the Allies giving West Germany massive debt relief, allowing that country to recover and to attract new investment. That is exactly what is needed in Rwanda, Mozambique, Honduras, and many, many other countries.

The project of canceling the debts of the poorest nations in the world now has the backing of many of the largest Christian denominations, and the articulate support of a good many economists, bankers and others who know their way around the financial world. Of course it will demand an outlook on life totally different to those which have ruled the worlds of international financing. But there is no reason to suppose that attitudes cannot be changed. Just as the conscience of the world was stung by the apartheid regime in South Africa, and the world finally got together and persuaded the authorities there to think again, so it is time that the conscience of the world should be stung by the crippling burden and enslavement of millions, and that the world should get together and say to its financial leaders that it is time to think again. It is not as though the cost would be enormous to the richer countries. The total cost of remitting the debts of the poorest countries, as calculated by the Jubilee 2000 movement, comes to around the same as is spent in the USA each year on going to the cinema.

This project towers above everything else that is planned for the Millennium, both because it is so sorely needed, and because it has the fingerprints of the gospel of Jesus all over it. Quite frankly, it makes the posturings of postmodernity look cheap, tawdry and irrelevant in comparison. If the historical Jesus is to come off the pages of the New Testament and into the postmodern world, then it is with symbolic actions like this that he will be recognised. What better way of declaring that Jesus is Lord and Caesar is not, that Jesus is Lord and Mammon is not?

And when better than the Millennium? If we are to celebrate the birth of Jesus, even if we get the date slightly wrong, what better way than through the acting out of his message of love and forgiveness?

All such actions are genuine moments of revelation, of apocalypse. They are symbolic actions which actually and truly unveil the loving presence of the creator God. They are also actions which challenge the rival world-views which declare that such a thing is impossible. There is no reason in the world's terms – in modernity or postmodernity – why one should cancel debts. If you have people in your power, why not keep them there? Debt cancellation is inexplicable in terms of Marx, Nietzsche or Freud. Nor can the postmodern critique touch it. It is a sign of hope, of love, of the gospel. It reveals, it unveils, the fact that there is another God to the gods worshipped in the world; another way of being human to the ways we have tried so often. If we were to cancel the debts of our two-thirds world brothers and sisters, we would find that a good many of their other problems would begin to be solved as well, since several major social and political ills are fostered in an atmosphere of enslavement. And if all this were to begin to happen, perhaps the beneficiaries would be driven to use apocalyptic language again in the way that the biblical writers used it. The sun, the moon and the stars would sing for joy.

Conclusion

It is Jesus, not Caesar, who is Lord and Saviour. It is Jesus, not Mammon, who makes the world go round. The challenge before us at the Millennium is to seek, through the work of the gospel, to bring this saving, healing, liberating announcement to bear on the world in every way we can. The message of the Millennium should be that the principalities and powers that still tyrannize this sorry old world are not in fact its rightful lord, and that Jesus is. That, as we saw, is exactly what the dating system of Dionysius the Insignificant was designed to say. That is why we are having a Millennium in the first place. The more we find ways of expressing and embodying this in actual life and work, in institutions and families and individual lives, the more we will be forging a way through the current mood of *fin de siècle* postmodern pessimism and out into a new and better way of living, a fresh start.

I can imagine some people, maybe even some Christians, saying that this Millennium business is all a mistake, and that we shouldn't go along with it. I wouldn't suggest for a moment that they were thereby being disloyal to Jesus. But I would suggest that they were missing out on the best chance we have had for many generations to lead the way spiritually, socially, and culturally, and to do so with the gospel itself. Modernity has run out of steam; the paradoxes of postmodernity are fun to play with, but end up swallowing their own tail, and, like the Cynic philosophy of old, offer no solution to the world's ills. I believe we have an enormous opportunity, as we approach the new Millennium, for serious and joyful mission to the postmodern world, for the creation of a post-postmodern world in which human beings are honored and valued, not exploited and oppressed. I believe this because I believe in Jesus, and in the new world which began with his resurrection.

For those who join me in this faith, the calling is clear. To those who do not, I simply ask, Is this not the way we should go? And if our own local and personal efforts may sometimes appear, when seen in global or

cosmic terms, small or useless, don't forget the nick-
name Dionysius gave himself: the Insignificant. Sometimes it is precisely the insignificant things – a baby conceived in the womb of a Galilean girl; a piece of broken
bread and a sip of wine; a hand raised in a risky vote for
justice and mercy – that turn out to be the most significant things in the world.

Appendix

Jubilee 2000 Contact Addresses

The Jubilee 2000 movement may be contacted at:

UK: Jubilee 2000 Coalition, PO Box 100, London, SE1 7RT, UK; 0171 401 9999. E-mail: mail@jubilee2000uk.org; website: http://www.jubilee2000uk.org

USA: Jubilee 2000/USA, 222 East Capitol St., NE, Washington, DC, USA, 20003-1036; (202) 783-3566.
E-mail: coord@j2000usa.org; website: www.j2000usa.org/j2000

Canada: Inter-Church Coalition on Africa, 129 St Clair Ave, W. Toronto, Ontario, Canada, M4V 1N5; (416) 927-1124.
E-mail: iccaf@web.net

Australia: Grant Hill, TEAR Australia, PO Box 289, Hawthorn, 3122 Victoria, Australia; (03) 9819 1900.
E-mail: grant@tear.org.au

New Zealand: Cathy Ross, NZ Church Missionary Society, 1/63 Fancourt St, Meadowbank, Auckland 1005, New Zealand; (64) 9 5286755. E-mail: tearvic@ozemail.com.au

ACKNOWLEDGEMENTS

I am grateful to several people and organizations who helped me to think all this through. Lichfield Cathedral, whose Dean I have been for the last five years, has been planning for the year 2000, not just to celebrate the Millennium but to commemorate the 1300th anniversary of the Cathedral's original foundation on Christmas Day 700. The Massachusetts Bible Society invited me to lecture in October 1998 on the subject of the Millennium in relation to the nature of apocalyptic. Christian Aid, not least its Lichfield representatives, Michael and Jan Hawkes, have helped me face the challenge of Jubilee 2000. And my old friend Brian Walsh has continued to stir my imagination with the task of understanding and responding to contemporary Western culture. I am grateful to them all, and cheerfully absolve them all from responsibility for my arguments or conclusions. I must also thank Dr Carey Newman of Westminster John Knox Press, Louisville, Kentucky, and Mr Simon Kingston of SPCK, London, England, for their enthusiasm for this project and their help in bringing it swiftly to birth.

This book serves as an affectionate and grateful gift to Coventry Cathedral, whose Canon Theologian I have been since 1992. I have much enjoyed my connection with that historic place, whose own unique symbolism has done so much, over the years, to speak to contemporary society of a different way of being human.

Tom Wright